KIN GROUPS
AND
SOCIAL
STRUCTURE

KIN GROUPS AND SOCIAL STRUCTURE

ROGER M. KEESING
Australian National University

HOLT, RINEHART AND WINSTON
New York, Chicago, San Francisco, Atlanta
Dallas, Montreal, Toronto, London, Sydney

Library of Congress Cataloging in Publication Data

Keesing, Roger M.   1935–
    Kin groups and social structure.

    Bibliography: p. 155
    1. Kinship.   2. Social structure.   I. Title.
GN480.K43   301.42′1   74–16008

ISBN 0-03-012846-3

PREFACE

Social groups based on kinship and descent are centrally important in the lives of tribal peoples. Anthropologists have been documenting and analyzing them for almost a century. Through nineteenth century evolutionary studies, American historicalist anthropology, British studies of social structure, and recently even continental structuralism, a concern with clans and lineages, with patrilineal and matrilineal, has been a continuing theme. The literature on kinship and descent is massive and technical.

In these days when tribesmen are listening to transistor radios and voting in elections, and when Third World nations and urban ghettos increasingly command anthropological attention, study of the details of kin group organization smacks a bit of scholasticism. However, kinship studies have a continuing fascination; and many of the classic problems are still not clearly resolved. Through the years these problems have drawn the attention not only of the greats in kinship studies —such scholars as Morgan, Rivers, Lowie, Radcliffe-Brown, Evans-Pritchard, Fortes, Eggan, Murdock, and Lévi-Strauss—but also of many whose anthropological fame has come mainly from other studies— Tylor, Durkheim, Boas, Kroeber, Malinowski, Sapir, Linton, White, and Mead.

Acquiring a measure of technical competence in kinship theory is crucial in cultural anthropology, even for the student who does not aspire to professional specialization in kinship studies. Without such competence, one cannot read with comprehension the major anthropological journals such as *Man, American Anthropologist, Journal of Anthropological Research, Ethnology, Africa,* and *L'Homme*; and one cannot adequately understand anthropological monographs on tribal peoples. Without it, one cannot understand the development of theory in social anthropology—for many fundamental issues about human social life have been debated in the arena of kinship. Finally, whatever kind of field work one does in a tribal or peasant society, the social structure must be described as a framework for any analysis to follow.

To provide such a level of competence for graduate students and advanced undergraduates requires greater detail than general introductory texts provide; yet there have been few attempts to give a higher-level introduction. The chapters that follow should, if they are carefully studied, equip the student to read monographs and journal articles with considerable sophistication. In a field where technical controversies have long raged, where definitions are endlessly argued, and where each specialist has his particular prejudices, there is no such thing as a "standard" version of kinship theory. My own biases are obviously expressed in the chapters that follow, but they are tempered so that alternative views can be understood and interpolated.

The student who wants to explore an alternative synthesis of kinship theory may find it useful to go to another book that covers similar ground. Fox (1967), Goodenough (1970), Sahlins (1968), and Buchler and Selby (1968) are likely to prove helpful. However, the next step in going seriously and substantially beyond the introduction that I (or any other single scholar) can provide is to begin to read classic papers in the field. Graburn (1971) includes an excellent collection of readings, with useful introductions and a good bibliography. Using that book in conjunction with this one would add both technical sophistication and historical perspective. Other useful collections of technical papers have been edited by Bohannan and Middleton (1968a, 1968b) and Goody (1968). In addition, the interested reader can explore the references given in the text. An attempt has been made to cite the clearest statements and most representative examples of the various theoretical positions presented. Another useful way to work one's way further into kinship theory would be to read the generally excellent technical reviews in the *International Encyclopedia of the Social Sciences*. The sections written by Eggan, Goody, Dumont, Goodenough, and Marshall (each cited in the bibliography under 1968) are particularly likely to be helpful.

There is, inevitably, a difficult line to draw in describing kin groups and social structure. Where does this subject stop and another begin? I have focused mainly on descent groups, and only secondarily on family and domestic groups. And I have left marriage systems largely to the side, except as they relate to the structure and interweaving of descent groups and the nature of alliance systems. How I view the connectedness between kinship groups, marriage systems, and other facets of social structure can be seen in wider context but lesser detail in my recent introduction to social anthropology, *New Perspectives in Cultural Anthropology* (1971). The chapters that follow represent an expansion and elaboration of the argument presented there, and I am indebted to Holt, Rinehart and Winston, Inc., for permission to adapt long passages from that work.

It is all too easy, in summarizing kin group organization in the primitive world, to build typological pigeonholes ("patrilineal," "matrilineal," "cognatic" . . .) into which the range of tribal social forms can be classified. Easy, but misleading. First of all, one risks overlooking the way social forms represent adaptive solutions to ecological and organizational problems. Second, one is prone to classify on the basis of a few formal and ideological features, and to end up putting in the same pigeonhole systems that are only superficially similar, and separating systems that are only superficially dissimilar. And third, one is tempted to characterize a whole society on the basis of some single idealized formal rule or principle, overlooking more subtle alternative organizational principles. In the study of social organization, it has been all too easy and common to oversimplify and idealize social groupings and categories that are complex and variable.

Here, I will try to avoid the worst traps of "butterfly collecting" (Leach 1962b) by placing the development and diversification of kin groupings in evolutionary and ecological perspective; and, while outlining comparatively the formal principles of kin group organization, by emphasizing and illustrating the internal complexity and diversity of actual societies.

My intellectual debts in the study of kin groups are diverse, but I would like to acknowledge a special debt to Ward Goodenough, Edmund Leach, David Maybury-Lewis, Rodney Needham, Douglas Oliver, and Harold Scheffler.

For helpful suggestions for extensive revision of the first draft of the book, I am indebted to C. O. Frake, Ward Goodenough, Nelson Graburn, and Stephen Tyler. Shelley Schreiner has given generously of advice and support during writing and revision; and Peggy Middendorf has lent patient and skillful editorial assistance.

R. M. K.

CONTENTS

KIN GROUPS
AND
SOCIAL
STRUCTURE

1
KINSHIP
IN
EVOLUTIONARY
PERSPECTIVE

For decades, anthropologists studying kinship gave little thought to our primate ancestors or to our distant cousins, the modern apes and monkeys. The speculations of nineteenth century cultural evolutionists about primitive promiscuity and other dark doings in the ancient past had given way to a critical skepticism about conjectural history. Moreover, the cultural theory of the Boasian tradition emphasized the plasticity of humans to the molding of their cultural impress and the diversity of ways of life in different times and places. The biological heritage all humans share as products of evolution was submerged from view (Freeman 1969).

With modern studies of primates in the wild, and new views of the evolution of behavior patterns, we have realized that *Homo sapiens* embodies a cumulation of biological patterning; we are not simply creatures of culture. Studies of primate ethology have dramatically underlined both the evolutionary continuities that link us with our primate past, and the new patterns that are distinctively human.

NONHUMAN PRIMATE SOCIAL ORGANIZATION

First of all, modern primates live in *groups*. Characteristically primate bands or troops include some 10 to 80 animals. In most primate species the composition of groups is quite stable; but among some of the apes—especially chimpanzees, our closest relatives—groups are relatively open, and individual animals may move from one group to another.

A second characteristic feature of primate social organization is that bands occupy territories (or, more precisely, *home ranges*; though a primate band occupies and forages in a particular area, its members usually do not defend that area by force against incursions by other bands; such a defense is what, in the technical parlance of ethologists, defines a true "territory").

Third, primate groups are internally structured. One axis of differentiation is based on sex, another on age. Thus, adult males play a different part in the group than do adult females; juveniles of each sex have other parts to play; and infants form still another category. Another axis is one of dominance: one or more adult males characteristically exercise dominance and leadership. They enjoy priority in sexual access, feeding, and the like; and they command deference. Dominance is strikingly important in some primate species, notably baboons, whose ground-living adaptations have been particularly interesting to students of human evolution; but for our much closer relatives, the gorillas and chimpanzees, dominance is much less extreme.

The primary stable grouping within the band is the unit of mother and young. Females are sexually active only cyclically and seasonally (they come in "heat" or estrus). There is no regular and stable association of male and female as mates (a "pair bond"), as in the human family (except among gibbons, where the similarity to the human "nuclear family" is only superficial). In some species there seem to be inhibitions of mother-son mating, but beyond this there is nothing approaching the human incest taboo.

Importantly, among modern primates there is no sharing of food and no division of labor in foraging. Each animal, once it matures beyond infancy, must seek its own food. Interestingly, one of the few partial exceptions— among our close relatives the chimpanzees—is an almost ritualized sharing of meat from a kill, which is relatively infrequent.

We can thus reasonably infer that the primate ancestors from which we and living apes are descended occupied home ranges and lived in social groups structured by sex, age, and dominance, within which mother-infant pairs were important units. We can infer that there were no larger "family" units with permanently associated males, and that there was no division of labor in foraging. Each band was probably a self-contained and self-sufficient group within which mating and reproduction took place. How much movement between bands took place is a matter of speculation, but patterned "political" relations between bands were probably minimal.

THE EVOLUTION OF HOMINID SOCIAL ORGANIZATION

In the long period during which early hominids evolved, two major developments in the internal organization of groups took place. One was pair-bonding: a male mate joined the unit of mother-plus-infant on a more-or-less stable basis. This involved a complex of biological changes and cultural adaptations. A crucial change was development of more-or-less continual sexual receptivity of the female, making mating possible all year and at any time, not simply during estrus. Marked prolonging of infantile dependence so that a child did not become self-sufficient for a number of years was associated with the development of culture; an infant now had a vast amount to learn to become equipped for adult life.

A second major development in the direction of human social organization was *sharing*, especially sharing of food. This created a *division of labor*. Old and young could be dependent on able-bodied adults for food. Males and females could specialize in and divide the critical subsistence tasks.

Just how, when, and why these changes took place has been a matter of some controversy. The simplest explanation is that the evolution of pair-bonding and of a division of labor by sex were linked together: male mate, specialized as hunter and provider and protector, and female mate specialized as food collector and child-rearer, would have served complementary functions. But others, questioning the assumptions of male dominance that underlie this interpretation, have suggested that a division of labor between mother and male offspring, or between male and female children of the same mother, could have served the same ecological functions. Pair-bonding could thus have been later, and secondary.

At some point in the restructuring of the internal relations of hominid bands, mating between mother and sons, between sons and daughters, and (possibly later) between fathers and daughters, was prohibited. Just how and why *incest taboos* originated have long been favorite topics of anthropological speculation.

Along with pair-bonding and a sexual division of labor, though perhaps much later, came a restructuring of both internal and external relations of bands. As long as a band, hunting and gleaning in a home range, was self-sufficient, and mating and reproduction took place within the band, human society was hardly possible. What was needed to create political interdependence on a wider scale and to make possible the development of regional cultures was intermarriage between bands. Lévi-Strauss (1949) argued that a rule of band *exogamy*, or out-marriage, must have been a central early invention best viewed as a kind of collective incest taboo. The males of a band, by renouncing sexual access to their own females and establishing a kind of social contract with surrounding bands, could gain access to mates from the outside. Through exogamy and intermarriage, political interdependence between bands and the emergence of a common language and culture would become possible. Although this has something of the quality of a just-so story, at some stage in the protohuman or human past such webs of out-mating between local groups were spun.

Just how and at what stage these elements of social organization emerged we do not know. We probably never will, though our guesses will be progressively refined. We presume that the development of a primal "family" and a division of labor constituted part of a biological and cultural complex of early man, probably long before the full development of language and symbolization. With the elaboration of linguistic codes and symbolic systems, within perhaps the last 100,000 or even 50,000 years, presumably came a conceptualization of kinship ties between individuals, families, and bands.

SOCIAL ORGANIZATION OF HUNTERS AND GATHERERS

Early humans come more clearly into view in the Upper Paleolithic (the last 35,000 years). Here we have not only richer archeological records, but also ethnographic accounts of those hunting and gathering peoples that survived into modern times. Working from reconstructions of the past and from modern ethnographic descriptions, anthropologists have devoted far more attention in the last decade than ever before to uncovering the ecology, social organization, and world view of hunters and gatherers (Lee and DeVore 1968; Service 1966; Bicchieri 1972; Coon 1971).

Some years ago, anthropologists thought that the basic mode of social organization among many or most hunting and gathering peoples was the "patrilocal band" (Steward 1955). Bands of fairly small size (50 to 100) were seen as controlling territories. It would be ecologically adaptive to have groups of men hunting together on a territory they had all known since boyhood. Hence, rules that (1) a man must marry a girl from a different territory and (2) the wife goes to live in the husband's territory, would create ecologically effective bands and link them together by webs of kinship. (Since clusters of men related through males would then comprise a band, it would be a minimal conceptual jump to an ideology of "patrilineal descent," where people are seen as related to one another and their territory through a chain of male ancestors.) In other hunting and gathering societies where sparse and scattered resources or other ecological factors militated against collective enterprise in bands, organization in fragmented nuclear families would be adaptive. The Shoshoni of the western United States provide a vivid example.

CASE 1: SHOSHONI SOCIAL ORGANIZATION

The Shoshoni of Nevada, and other Shoshonean-speaking peoples of the Great Basin (Ute and Paiute), had an extremely simple and fragmented social organization, classed by Steward (1955) as a "family level of socio-cultural integration."

The Shoshoni environment was extremely arid, harsh, diversified, and unpredictable. It included desert and near-desert, lakes and streams, high pine forests, and a range of intermediate settings at different elevations. Winter was cold and severe, summer hot and dry. The sparse food resources—mainly rabbits and other small game and, even more important, pine nuts and other wild vegetable foods—were scattered and undependable.

In such a setting, settlement by man was very sparse (one person to every 5, 10, or even 50 or 100 square miles). Mobility was necessary; no permanent settlements were possible, and only tiny groups could make ends meet in the business of subsistence.

The Shoshoni and their neighbors developed an adaptation whereby nuclear families or polygynous families (a man and two or more wives) lived alone for most of the year—perhaps 80 percent of the time. They moved in pursuit of food, following the seasons. Only when resources were temporarily abundant (fish in streams, pine nuts in forests) did several families live together. In winter they sometimes camped together, living largely on whatever dried nuts and seeds they had been able to store. At other times they joined together in communal hunts for rabbit or antelope. Such gatherings were times for dancing and collective religious rites.

Families were exogamous. Characteristically, however, marriage alliances would be worked out between two families so that when a young man from one family married a young woman from another, the younger children of the two families would also marry when the time came. When a man took two or more wives, they were supposed to be sisters. If a spouse died, his or her surviving sibling was expected, if possible, to marry the widow or widower. The several families united by such marriages would usually be the ones that coordinated their movements so as to group together seasonally when resources permitted (Steward 1955).

The "patrilocal band" model has been cast in some doubt by recent studies of modern hunters and gatherers that show band groups to be quite diverse and heterogeneous in composition, reveal considerable mobility between bands, and indicate that bands hunt extensively on one another's territories (Lee and DeVore 1968). Moreover, as Lévi-Strauss (1949) has pointed out, in the Paleolithic world it is quite possible that marriages were based not on the negative rule that a man must marry a woman in a different band, but on positive rules of marital alliance where bands exchanged women (see Cases 16 and 17).

The variability and flexibility that have turned up increasingly in the social organization of modern hunter-gatherers[1] are well illustrated by the !Kung Bushmen.

CASE 2: !KUNG BUSHMAN SOCIAL ORGANIZATION

The !Kung Bushmen are hunters and gatherers living in the forbidding Kalahari desert of southern Africa. The arid environment permits survival only in small, scattered bands. Bushman bands, ranging in size from about 20 to 60, are spread over some 10,000 square miles; the total population is only about 1000.

Each band has a territory. Within a territory, rights to gather wild vegetable foods—the everyday staples on which existence depends—are limited to band members. Water is another scarce resource, and each band has primary rights to the waterhole or holes on which they depend (though outsiders may use water with permission). Hunters of large animals may cross into other band territories quite freely in pursuit of game. If a band's waterhole goes dry, its component families move temporarily to live with other bands where they have relatives.

Each band is made up of a cluster of families. Some are nuclear families, related to one another by bonds of kinship. However, some are augmented into "extended families" by the presence of one or more married children and their families. Some of the households are polygynous (a man with more than one wife).

Bands are not exogamous by rule. Marriage is forbidden within the nuclear family, between certain close kin, and between a man and a girl whose name is the same as his mother's. (There is a limited set of names for men and women, transmitted along family lines; name sharing is taken to imply distant kinship.) Some marriages do take place within a band. When a man takes his first wife, he goes to reside with his bride's father until two or three children have been born (doing "bride service," and by his hunting contributing to the larder of his father-in-law and his band). Since marriage often takes place well before the bride reaches puberty this may cover a span of eight or ten years, during which the husband is absent from his band. After that, the husband may take his wife and children back to his father's band, or may choose to remain with his wife's people.

Each band has a headman. He has formal authority over the disposition of a band's resources and its movements, but his political powers are in fact quite limited. Group action is usually based on a consensus of its members. In some ways the headman's stewardship is symbolic. His *de facto* power depends on his personal skills at leading, organiz-

---

[1] Some experts believe that much of this fluidity is a product of modern colonialism and the resulting fragmentation, disruption, imposed peace, and depopulation.

ing, planning, and maintaining internal harmony. Headship of the band passes through family lines, from a headman to his oldest son.

Internal conflicts, as between a headman and his younger brother or another kinsman, are resolved either by the dissident member moving to another band where he has relatives; or by the dissident faction splitting off to form a new band. Relatives-by-marriage may join a band and enjoy equal rights with persons born into the band, but these privileges lapse if they leave. The rights of a person born into the band to live in its territory and share in its resources remain even though he or she may live elsewhere; the option to return continues to be open (Marshall 1959, 1960, 1965).

Given the small groups, sparse population, mobility, and loose relationship to territories imposed by hunting and gathering technology, kinship served only limited social ends. Kinship, traced through father and mother, tied together people in the same band and different bands, fostering unity within the band and peaceful relations with outside individuals and groups. In such webs of kinship and intermarriage between bands lay potential solutions to new organizational and ecological problems that awaited man with the dawn of food producing.

As the technology of food producing spread across the primitive world, social life was transformed over much of Africa, Eurasia, the Americas, and the Pacific. In marginal areas where agriculture was unfeasible, pastoral adaptations were elaborated. In regions more favorable to cultivation, including tropical rain forests, diverse ways of life based primarily on agriculture evolved, in adaptation to the ecological niches men could now exploit with new control.

In this process of diversification and adaptation, which Sahlins (1960) has likened to "adaptive radiation" in biological evolution, man's old "invention" of kinship reckoning assumed central importance in solving a new set of organizational problems.

The new problems came partly from larger numbers of people living more closely, and with less mobility. They came partly from the necessity for collective action by larger, cohesive groups—and from the corresponding need to control conflict between these groups and tie them together into a wider system. They came partly from new "things,"—land, livestock, and other property—and from how rights over these "things" had to be transmitted across generations and adjusted to the whims of demography.

The diverse forms of kin grouping in the tribal world that have so preoccupied anthropologists can partly be viewed as varying solutions to these and related problems in different environmental settings, adaptations to a wide range of ecological niches. In the sections to follow, various modes of kin grouping in the tribal world and the pressures that seem to shape them will be examined.

Kinship, then, is the dominant mode of forming the larger groupings central in social, economic, and political life in societies of the "middle range" of social and technological scale and complexity. With the urban revolution, kinship as an organizing principle has become overshadowed by ties of class, occupational specialization, and community. To modern urbanites, kinship ties are bonds within and between families. The range and importance of kinship networks in urban settings are turning out to be greater, in many cases, than anthropologists realized a decade or two ago. Kinship ties help to weave the lives of individual city dwellers together; but lineages, clans, and other groups formed on kinship lines no longer define a person's place in the society.

We will turn momentarily to the ecological and organizational challenges that confronted humans as food producers—and to the ways kinship provided avenues of solution. But first, we need to clarify what anthropologists mean by "groups," and how they relate to cultural categories. And we need to look more closely at what *kinship* is about; for we tend to assume too casually that our ideas about "blood relatives" are shared by other peoples.

2
KINSHIP AND DESCENT

CATEGORIES, GROUPS, AND CORPORATIONS

If we are going to look seriously at kin groups, we had best begin with a careful idea of what *groups* are. Perhaps more theorists of kinship over the years have come to grief or caused confusion by losing track of the difference between social groups and cultural categories than by any other conceptual flaw.

First of all, I use "culture" to refer to an ideational system, a system of *knowledge*. Culture, in Ward Goodenough's phrase, consists of "standards for deciding what is, . . . what can be, . . . how one feels about it, . . . what to do about it, and . . . how to go about doing it" (1961:522). "Society," or social structure, consists of the groupings and arrangements of people; "culture" refers to the ideas, meanings, and knowledge, conscious and unconscious, people share.

The distinction between society and culture enables us to see a contrast between *cultural categories* and *social groups*. A cultural category is a set of entities in the world (people, things, events, supernaturals) that are classed as similar for some purposes, because they have in common one or more culturally relevant attributes. Thus trees, weeds, bachelors, and left-handed baseball pitchers are categories in American culture. As categories, they exist in people's *conceptual* worlds; the category "cow" does not eat grass. Note also that not all of them have one-word labels in our language. Nor are they sets of entities we keep in separate "chunks" in our conceptual world. Rather, they are sets we *draw mental lines around* in particular contexts. Women who wear size seven dresses comprise a relevant category in only a very few contexts (mainly for people who make or sell dresses, while they happen to be at work). Thus any single entity can be classed, in varying contexts, as belonging to dozens of different cultural categories. A category of human beings, grouped conceptually because of some socially relevant features they share in common (like "men" or "warriors" or "descendants of ancestor X"), we can call a *social category*.

A *social group*, on the other hand, consists of actual warm-blooded human beings who recurrently interact in an interconnected set of roles. Thus groups can be distinguished from forms of aggregation, such as crowds or gatherings, whose interaction is temporary and limited. Members of a social group need not all interact face-to-face, though such *primary groups* are common in the small-scale communities anthropologists usually study. What defines a group is its internal organization, the articulation of its members in a set of interconnected roles. Thus the stockholders of General Motors comprise a *secondary group*. Although most of its members do not interact with one another, they are bound into a group through their relationships with the management.

Who *belongs to* a group is seldom neatly defined by some cultural principle like being descended from the same ancestor, or being the right age or social class. Such membership in a social category usually defines *eligibility* for membership in a group. Whether an eligible person actually takes part in a group is likely to depend on the circumstances of life history, on economic interests and resources, and on personal choice.

To illustrate some basic points about categories and groups, we will look at a hypothetical example from our own society—one that parallels closely the kinship-based categories and groups of tribal societies.

Imagine that three generations ago, in a New England community, ten people organized and founded a music festival which has gone on ever since. Priority for tickets to the festival now goes to the Patrons of the festival, who comprise all those descendants of the ten founders who take part in meetings and maintain an active interest. Many of the descendants *eligible* to be Patrons have, of course, moved away and lost touch. But if they ever moved back, they could become active again; and if they happened to visit on the day of the performance a good seat would always be found for them. At any performance there will also be persons in the audience who come as guests of Patrons, or who are simply filling the remaining seats.

What sorts of social units have we here? First, all descendants of the founders, whether Patrons or those who have moved away or lost interest, form a *social category*. Their descent status makes them *eligible* to activate a set of rights. Second, those descendants who are Patrons comprise a *corporate group*, which ultimately controls the activities of the festival (and whose members enjoy the attendant privileges, though they may well not turn up at a particular performance). Finally, the audience actually attending a performance comprises a *gathering*. But if they gathered in some more organized fashion to perform a common task (to erect a new stage, for example), we could call the mixed bunch who actually came an *action group* or *task group*. The anthropological literature is full of confusions about "clans" and "lineages" and "kindreds" where these distinctions between groups and categories, corporations and action groups, have been blurred or overlooked.

KINSHIP AS A CULTURAL PRINCIPLE
AND SOCIAL MECHANISM

What are relations of kinship? The question seems clear and simple enough. On the one hand, we have intuitions about "blood" relationships—as natural, as connections of shared substance, as "thicker than water." Kinship is so basic as to be taken for granted. On the other hand, there are all those genealogical diagrams, those triangles and circles and lines anthropologists have been drawing for decades. Kinship in tribal societies is obviously those vertical lines between parents and children, those braces connecting siblings.

But things are not quite that simple. Our intuitions are *cultural* intuitions: we cannot assume that they are shared by Zuni Indians or Trobriand Islanders. And what those lines on genealogical diagrams mean is a matter of great current controversy. At issue are the most basic assumptions about kinship and the study of kinship (Beattie 1964; Schneider 1972; Needham 1972; Scheffler 1974).

We cannot explore the controversy in full detail; and by taking a particular position we risk too partisan a presentation. But it is important to begin with an idea of what the issues are. In the process, the author's own prejudices will be evident. But the student should bear in mind that many experts read the same evidence in very different ways.

Humans everywhere observe the same processes of sex and reproduction. A female has sexual intercourse, one or many times, with one man or many. She never becomes pregnant without sex; but she only sometimes becomes pregnant after having intercourse. Once she is pregnant, it is ultimately obvious that she is, and that the infant is connected to her by the most physical of bonds—by the umbilical cord, by childbirth, by the milk of her breasts. But the connection of the one or several men who had intercourse with the mother, or were publicly believed to have done so, to the process of pregnancy and childbirth is far from obvious.

The physical evidence available to tribesmen regarding the contributions of the male and female sex partner to the process of pregnancy, and the resulting child, allows much room for cultural interpretation. The male deposits semen; and sometimes menstruation stops and pregnancy ensues (making probable the inference that the woman contributes "blood"—in some sense, and whatever blood means in that culture). That the genetic contributions of sperm and ovum are matching and equivalent is a recent scientific discovery hardly available to tribal peoples. Interpretations of pregnancy may in different cultures see the male as contributing seed, the female as contributing container or symbolic "earth" within which the seed sprouts; or the male as contributing bone (whitish, like semen), the female as contributing flesh (red, like blood); and so on—the range of possibility is wide.

Some peoples have reportedly denied that a man's sexual intercourse with the mother is a "cause" of pregnancy (notably the much-argued cases of Australian Aborigines and the Trobriand Islanders of Melanesia). Is this "ignorance of physical paternity," as some have claimed? Or does it represent religious dogma akin to that of virgin birth in Christianity? Or a kind of political statement about men and women? Does it represent a different religious interpretation of causality and "chance"? Is intercourse seen as a necessary but not sufficient precondition for pregnancy, with supernatural intervention needed to *vivify* (animate) the fetus? Anthropologists have had much room for debate, just as tribal peoples have had much room for cultural embroidery on observed biological events.

Moreover, every society must deal with sexual intercourse outside whatever bounds are considered legitimate. Women have sexual relations, sometimes or often, with men who are not socially and legally defined as the appropriate "fathers" for their children. In some societies, this is institutionalized to the point that a dead man is legally defined as the "father," or that a *woman* is defined as the "father" of children borne by a woman she has legally married (whose male sexual partners may be publicly recognized). All peoples must come to terms with the slippage between the men legitimately entitled to beget women's children and the men presumed actually to do so. This has left much room for anthropological debate as well, in terms of a gulf between "social" and "physical" kinship, or between *pater* (the legitimate social father) and *genitor* (the presumed physical begetter of the child).

What are we to make of all this? David Schneider and his students have recently argued that "kinship" is best seen as a purely cultural and symbolic construct substantially free of biological roots. How cultures conceptualize this realm is highly variable; and the symbolic systems of "kinship" are misunderstood from the outset if we think of them in genealogical terms (Schneider 1972).

What, then, distinguishes cultural conceptions of "kinship" such that we can carve out such a class of phenomena for comparative study? Why call it "kinship" at all? First of all, cultural conceptualizations of kinship connections apparently universally view them as natural and inalienable, and in some symbolic sense as a connection of substance. And sexual intercourse and reproduction serve as appropriate cultural symbols for this natural connectedness of substance. Yet in each culture, the structure of the symbolic realm, and the roles ordered in terms of kinship categories, must be analyzed in their own terms. To begin with a supposedly universal grid of genealogical connection is to distort the study of kinship at the outset.

An alternative position has been set out by Scheffler (1974). He argues that all, or almost all, cultures posit genealogical connections between *genitrix* (the physical mother) and child and also between *genitor* (the presumed physical father) and child. The connection between genitor and child may not be conceived as the same as that between genetrix and child, may be conceived as metaphysical rather than physical substance, or as spiritual influence:

> But in other respects both kinds of genealogical connection are held to be the same: both are regarded as necessary and complementary products of reproductive processes and both are regarded as inalienable; that is, once they are established they cannot be undone, and they cannot be established in any other way (Scheffler 1974:750).

As Scheffler makes clear, the social status characteristically associated with "fatherhood" in fact consists of component elements that can be separated and assigned to different people in less than ideal circumstances. Some of these components derive from being the presumed genitor; others from being mother's husband; others from feeding and caring for the child; and so on. So-called "social fathers" who are presumed not to be genitors are simply enacting some of these elements or "social identities" established by legal transactions or behavioral validation, not genealogical connection. The rights and duties, and the criteria for assuming each of the component social identities that together constitute the ideal bundle of "fatherhood," must of course be sorted out in each case.

Genealogical connections between parents and child are extended outward to connect ego (the point of reference) to the parents of ego's parents and to the children of ego's children; to connect ego to her or his siblings (by their genealogical connection to the same parents); and outward through parents' siblings to "collateral" relatives.

"Kinship," then, is the network of relationships created by genealogical connections, and by social ties (e.g., those based on adoption) *modelled on* the "natural" relations of genealogical parenthood.

Such conceptualization of kinship makes sense of a world-wide range of data, while not elevating the realm of cultural symbols to an autonomous level free of the constraints—ecological, sociological, cognitive, and bio-logical—that limit diversity. Freeman (1974), for example, has argued forcefully that kinship behavior in humans builds on evolutionarily-rooted biological patterns of mother-infant bonding. He argues that the tremendous psychological force of kin ties derives from these psychobiological roots. Kinship is, preeminently, a realm where mutual moral obligation prevails, where the "axiom of amity" (Fortes 1969) holds sway; but it is also a realm where ambivalence and conflict universally run against these moral tenets. Both amity and ambivalence, Freeman argues, are deeply rooted in our psychobiological nature and primal experience. But on these matters, the experts disagree sharply. At stake are not simply technical questions about kinship, but questions about the nature of human beings and the most basic elements of human behavior and social explanation. We cannot take time to explore them further. It is important to know, first, that in this field of kinship and social structure the experts differ on first principles, not simply on details; second, that these gulfs are widening, not narowing, in the recent literature; and third, that the issues are deep and important ones, even though kinship experts may seem to phrase their debate in terms of exotic and trivial detail.

Networks that connect individuals as relatives are apparently universally recognized and universally accorded social importance. Note that every individual, other than full siblings, has a unique array of relatives, on mother's and father's sides. Kinship ties serve, then, to define the unique position of each individual in her or his social world—to establish strands of mutual amity and obligation in that individual's own group and in other groups (Fortes 1969).

When a particular individual becomes the focal point of attention (as when he or she is born, initiated, married, buried, or whatever), his or her relatives can gather around in support, celebration, or mourning. But the group so formed is always temporary, and cannot act on a day-to-day basis or form an ongoing corporation. Each individual has a unique circle of relatives; and any person belongs to many such circles, not one. Your Uncle George is also someone else's father, another person's brother, still another person's cousin. George can act in each of these capacities on different occasions, but he cannot act in all of them all the time.

In almost every society, a person's circle of relatives plays some part in social life. Where they (or some of them, say, up to the distance of second cousins) are conceptually recognized as a cultural category, such a category has a special anthropological label: a *kindred* or *personal kindred* (Freeman 1961; Murdock 1960; W. E. Mitchell 1963).

An idealized kindred is diagrammed in Figure 1. This figure also shows the special anthropological conventions for diagramming kinship connections (Barnes 1967b), and hence provides a key to subsequent diagrams.

The descending arrows on Figure 1 indicate that the descendants of

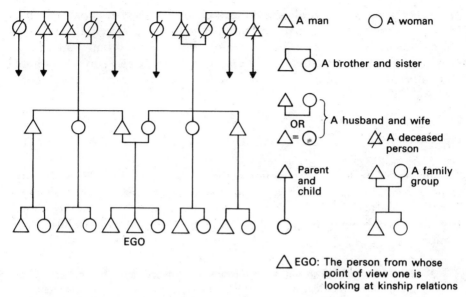

A man   A woman

A brother and sister

OR

A husband and wife

A deceased person

Parent and child

A family group

EGO

EGO: The person from whose point of view one is looking at kinship relations

FIGURE 1   A Personal Kindred.

siblings of grandparents (or of great-grandparents and more distant relatives) may be included for some purposes within a kindred category. Since in real life families often include many siblings, not simply two, the actual kindred of a tribesman or tribeswoman may include dozens of relatives. The number who actually participate in kindred-based action groups may be much smaller (since many potential members live far away, have competing obligations, belong to the opposite political faction, etc.). The overlapping nature of kindreds, the fact that any individual may "belong" to a great many kindreds, prevents a kindred from serving as an effective corporate group. Groups are recruited from kindreds only sporadically—particularly when the person around whom it is defined is born, gets married, gives a feast, dies, or otherwise temporarily occupies center stage. (It has been pointed out that the kindred of an important leader may stay, in a sense, mobilized around him; and that in a local group where people marry "in" [i.e., an endogamous community, rather than an exogamous one] kindreds will tend to overlap so much that everyone is in everyone else's kindred.)

Such reckoning of kinship through father and mother, and out to a range of more distant kin—grandparents, cousins, and so on—was apparently an old cultural invention, as we have noted. In some hunting and gathering societies (such as the Kariera, Case 16), the conceptualization of local groups as related by spiritual connection to ancestors in the male (or rarely, female) line produced something approaching the descent-organized corporations to which we will now turn. But the burgeoning and elaboration of descent groupings, and of descent as a cultural principle, apparently followed the emergence of tribal food producing, and was closely tied with it. Once humans were able to live in larger, more stable groups, once they came to view land as a "thing," not simply as a territorial surface to hunt and gather on, new social problems were faced, and new cultural solutions emerged.

DESCENT

Tribal[1] food producers, particularly those who had become sedentary through Neolithic agriculture, faced a new set of organizational challenges. It will be useful to make these new problems explicit before we consider how the kin groupings of the tribal world provided adaptive solutions to them.

1. How will stable, strong local groups be formed, capable of acting as independent political units in the absence of any central government?
2. How will the relationship of people to land be defined? With Neolithic food producing, land tenure is no longer a matter of hunting territories. The soil itself has become vital to life; and Neolithic technology is usually incompatible with a fixed relationship between individuals and small partitioned tracts of land.
3. How will the relationships of people to land and other resources be maintained across generations, and how will they be adjusted to demographic fluctuations?
4. How will an individual have rights, safety, and allies in local groups other than his own?
5. How will political relations between local groups be maintained without a central government? And when feuding or warfare between groups begins, how can they be controlled?

The seeds of a solution, flexible and adaptive, lay in the band organization of hunters and gatherers. If a band-like local group could become more solidary, if its members could collectively hold title to land, and if ties of intermarriage and kinship could weave together members of different bands, a workable and neat solution to these problems would seem to have been available.

What was needed was a way to convert bands, with political rights over

---

[1] "Tribal" is a somewhat ambiguous term anthropologically. In the technical literature on political organization, a society has been classed as "tribal" if its members were food-producing, occupied a territory, shared a common language and culture, but had no overarching political organization beyond local kin groups. I use the term somewhat more generally to refer to small-scale, stateless societies subsisting predominantly by food-producing.

territories, into landowning *corporations*, or corporate groups. A corporation, in the tribal world as in the business world (and as with the Patrons of our hypothetical music festival), is a group of people who together *act as a single legal individual*. In the tribal world they usually act corporately with regard to an estate in land. Characteristically, a corporation has a name or some other symbolic expression of the way it acts as a legal individual, an undifferentiated unit, vis-à-vis outsiders—however differentiated its members may be from one another seen from inside the group. Seen from outside, in an important sense they are all One.

A corporation could meet these five major organizational problems of the tribal world. Its members can collectively hold title to land and other property. They can exploit their resources by cooperative labor (even though members may garden in smaller family units and may own the actual garden plots, as opposed to the land, separately). Corporations can, in their status as legal individuals, be unified political forces—can conduct litigation and make treaties, conduct feuds and wars, and enter into contracts. They are stable, since the corporation continues despite the death and replacement of individual members.

But how are such corporations to be formed and defined in the tribal world? Could it be achieved by simply conceptualizing the local band group or territorial unit as a corporation? Perhaps. But in the tribal world, a conceptual innovation was worked out that tied together the local solidarity of a territorial group with the symbolic solidarity of shared kinship.

The crucial conceptual innovation worked out in the tribal world is to define a social category, not with reference to a living person, but with reference to an *ancestor*. That is, only people descended from an ancestor in a particular way are members of the category. A rule defining a particular kind of descent sequence that specifies who is (and is not) a member of the category is a *descent rule*.

In reckoning descent, a people postulate a particular kind of chain of parent-child links between ancestor and descendants. Three principal kinds of chains or "descent constructs" (Scheffler 1966) are culturally recognized in the tribal world:

> *Patrilineal* (or "agnatic") descent, from an ancestor down through a series of male links (i.e., through the ancestor's son, his son's sons, his son's sons' sons, etc.);
> *Matrilineal* (or "uterine") descent, from an ancestress down through a series of female links (through daughter, daughter's daughter, etc.);
> *Cognatic* descent, from an ancestor or ancestress through a series of links that can be male or female, or any combination of the two.

Patrilineal and matrilineal descent, since each traces an unbroken chain of links of one sex, are classed together as *unilineal*. Cognatic descent, in contrast, defines a broadly inclusive category including both unilineal and nonunilineal descendants—what has been called a "cognatic stock." Patrilineal descent and matrilineal descent are diagrammed in Figures 2 and 3.

Note that the categories defined by patrilineal descent do not include only men, and that the categories defined by matrilineal descent do not include only women. Both brother and sister are members of their father's patrilincal descent group, but only the brother will pass this membership to his children. Both sister and brother are members of their mother's matrilineal descent group, but only the sister will pass this membership to her children (Figures 2 and 3).

A rule of unilineal descent (patrilineal or matrilineal) would seem an ideal solution to the problem of achieving discrete, solidary corporations. If a particular ancestor is defined as the founding or "apical" ancestor from whom descent is traced, and all unilineal descendants belong to that corporation, then membership is unambiguous. Cognatic descent does not, by itself, produce such neatness. A single individual belongs to many cognatic stocks (e.g., those of all eight great-grandparents), whereas he has only a single line of patrilineal ancestors. We will shortly see how other mechanisms are needed to make cognatic descent the basis of discrete, stable corporations.

Descent corporations, or "corporate descent groups," were a crucial development in the evolution of tribal societies. They provided an adaptive solution, in different ecological settings, to the problems of maintaining political order and defining rights over land and other resources across generations.

Note that to tie descent corporations together into a wider system, a rule that marriage cannot take place within a corporation—a rule of *descent*

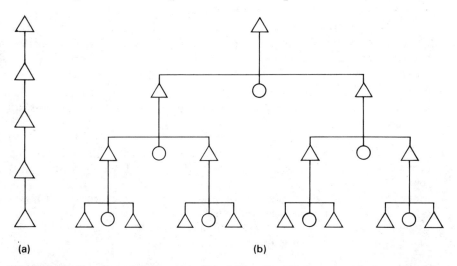

(a)   (b)

FIGURE 2   Patrilineal Descent.   (A) A Patrilineal Descent Construct. (B) A Patrilineal Descent Category. Note that it includes women, but not their children.

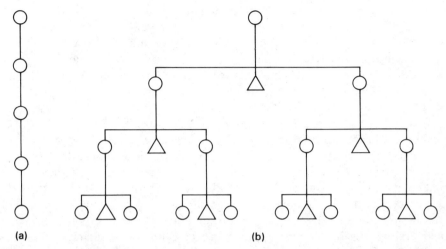

(a)   (b)

FIGURE 3   Matrilineal Descent.   (A) A Matrilineal Descent Construct. (B) A
Matrilineal Descent Category.

group exogamy—is crucially important (though we will see shortly some
systems where marriage within the corporation is permitted). Such a rule
of exogamy presumably represents an extension of the older principle of
band exogamy in hunting and gathering societies; and it serves the same
general functions of making groups interdependent and of weaving them
together with strands of kinship.

Patrilineal or matrilineal descent unambiguously defines who is eligible
for membership in a corporate descent group. Here, however, it is important
to note a potential gulf between being *entitled to* belong to a descent group
and actually exercising these rights actively. Recall, in our earlier example
of the New England music festival, that all the descendants of founders
were entitled to be Patrons, but that only some of them exercised their
potential rights in the group.

The gulf between descent entitlement and actual active corporation membership is crucial in making descent-based corporate groups ecologically
adaptive. Consider a hypothetical situation where garden land was equally
divided between six corporations whose membership was strictly defined by
patrilineal descent; and where the number of members in each group was
roughly equal. Imagine what would have happened demographically in a
generation or two: some groups would have proliferated, since many sons
had been born; in others, with more daughters and few sons, population
would have dwindled (these groups will mainly have been supplying wives
to the proliferating groups). Gross imbalances between population and
resources would quickly arise. *Unilineal descent systems must always include
some mechanism for redistributing population in relationship to resources
or for redistributing resources.* Various mechanisms operate in different

societies to achieve balance between humans and resources, including warfare, splitting off of new groups, and so on. A crucial recurring solution is to use the gulf between descent entitlement and actual active corporation membership, so that some people live and garden (or herd) in groups where they do not have the "official" descent credentials, using ties of kinship, marriage, political alliance, or friendship. Such flexibility can be crucial in maintaining an ecological balance of humans to resources.

This gulf in unilineal descent systems between entitlement and active membership can also help us to understand how cognatic descent operates in the tribal world. When, in the late 1950s and early 1960s, anthropologists belatedly began to realize the importance of cognatic descent, they noted that cognatic descent categories are too broadly inclusive to produce discrete corporate groups. As we have seen, an individual is cognatically descended from four grandparents, eight great-grandparents, and so on. Everyone belongs to many partly overlapping descent categories—seemingly an unwieldy way to form separate corporations. But as we will see, if only certain ancestors are relevant to descent reckoning, and if patterns of residence, life history, or personal choice are used to narrow down each individual's commitment to a single corporation, discrete cognatic descent groups can be formed. Furthermore, in societies where corporations are formed unilineally, cognatic descent from the apical ancestor is often used as well to confer secondary interests in a corporation.

This usefully underlines the way two or more principles of descent can be used in the same society for different or complementary purposes. Usually only one mode of descent is used to form descent corporations; and if other forms are culturally recognized, they are used to define who is entitled to secondary or different sorts of rights. The Tallensi of Ghana, a "classic" case in anthropology (Fortes 1945, 1949), will serve to illustrate.

CASE 3: THE TALLENSI OF GHANA

Patrilineal descent among the Tallensi is a pervasive principle central in social life. Every Tallensi is a member of his or her father's patrilineal descent corporation. Being in this corporation is the cornerstone of a person's property rights, group participation, and religious life. Since Tallensi descent corporations are exogamous, a person's mother comes from a different corporation, and his two grandmothers from two others. Any individual can trace cognatic descent from the ancestors of many descent groups (Keesing 1970). These secondary ties of cognatic descent are also important. When sacrifice is made by descent group members to one of their ancestors, all of the *cognatic* descendants of that ancestor (that is, people descended from women of the descent group who married out into other groups) are entitled to be present and partake of the sacrifice. Such cognatic descendants also can exercise some secondary secular rights in the corporation. Thus, all patrilineal descendants of the founding ancestor of a corporation are, as it were, primary or "voting" members; the descendants of women primary members who married out have secondary, "nonvoting" interests. In fact the marriage rule does not merely prohibit marriage within the corporation; it prohibits marriage between any two people cognatically descended from the founding ancestor of the same corporation.

The Tallensi use still a third mode of descent reckoning: powers of witchcraft are believed to be passed from mother to daughter; and persons related by chains of matrilineal descent from the same ancestress have special rights and obligations toward one another. (Scheffler [1974] argues that this is a special mode of reckoning kinship, not descent.) We will see shortly how in some other societies, both patrilineal and matrilineal descent are used to form corporations, with each kind of corporation relevant in a different sphere of social life.

KINSHIP AND DESCENT:
SOME CONCEPTUAL CLARIFICATIONS

At this stage, it is worth making more clear some conceptual points regarding kinship and descent as cultural principles:

TABLE 1

KINSHIP	DESCENT
1. Defined with reference to an individual (ego) or pairs of individuals.	1. Defined with reference to an ancestor (or ancestress).
2. Universally important.	2. Culturally recognized only in some societies.
3. Normally bilateral, from the standpoint of an ego.	3. Connects (through relatedness to a common ancestor) only a limited class of ego's relatives.
4. Kinship relationships are relative; you are a son or a nephew only in relation to some particular person.	4. Descent status is, in a sense, absolute. You are, or are not, a member of a particular descent group.

When we say that a society or culture has a *rule of descent*, we mean that a particular descent construct—patrilineal, matrilineal, or cognatic—is used to define membership in a social group or category. (As with the

Tallensi, a people may recognize two or more of these modes of descent.) Many societies, as we will see, have no rule of descent; they do not accord any special significance to a special kind of genealogical chain between ancestors and the living. In some societies, descent has only minimal significance.

In societies where descent groupings are culturally relevant, bilateral kinship is also always recognized and always important. Kinship reckoning creates a network of relationships between a great many individuals. A rule of descent gives special meaning to a limited subset of these relationships; it thus carves out pieces of this network and gives them some special social significance.

The term "kinship" is used in anthropology in both narrow and broad senses—and that can lead to confusion. In the narrow sense, "kinship" refers to connections between parents and children (i.e., connections of *filiation*) and to the networks of relationship built out of these parent-child links. In this narrow sense, then, "kinship" contrasts with marriage and the relations of *affinity* (between in-laws) created by marriage; and it contrasts with *descent*. But anthropologists also use "kinship" in a broader, inclusive, sense to refer to the whole conceptual and social field relating to kinship, marriage, and descent. An anthropologist "studying kinship" is as likely to be studying a marriage system as a way of classifying relatives.

That ambiguity should not lead us into thinking that the people anthropologists study conceptualize both kinship and descent as comprising together a total "kinship system." As Scheffler (1974) argues, most peoples who use descent to form social groupings apparently conceptualize the network of kinship and the system of descent as separate and parallel systems (even though both of them are constructed out of filial—parent-child—links). The point may seem trivial, but it is not. If we look at social action among, say, the Tallensi, we see why. A Tallensi father may interact toward his son *either* as his father (based on kinship) or as a fellow descendant of the same patrilineal ancestors (based on descent). The social occasion defines the appropriate relationship (the latter would be relevant, for instance, when they are participating together in a sacrifice to the ancestors of their descent group). It should not surprise us that the same person may enact different roles toward us. My father, for example, was Chairman of the department in which I did my undergraduate major; so my diploma happens to have his signature on it. What can too easily confuse us in looking at the Tallensi is that the system of kinship-based roles and the system of descent-based roles both build on the filial links between father and son.

The distinction between *lineal* and *lateral* may need some clarification. We have seen that in every kinship system relationship is traced through both father and mother. Universally, father's brother and mother's brother are a person's relatives, and so are their children. Kinship reckoning, in other words, is always two sided—*bilateral*. One cluster of a person's relatives, roughly half of them, are on his or her father's side; they are his *patrilateral* kin. The others are on his mother's side, his *matrilateral* kin.

Where descent is traced unilineally, a potential confusion arises. Where descent is traced in the male line, some of a person's relatives on the father's side—but not all of them—are his or her *patrilineal* kin (Figure 4). Similarly, where descent is traced on the female line, some of ego's relatives on the mother's side are *matrilineal* (Figure 5). Patrilineal is more limited or exclusive than patrilateral (because many patrilateral kin are related through women); matrilineal is more limited or exclusive than matrilateral. This comes out most clearly if we look at ego's father's mother's descent group in a patrilineal descent system (who are patrilateral but not patrilineal

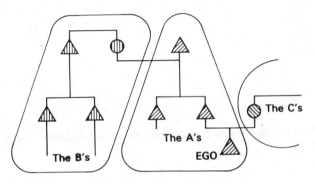

FIGURE 4   *Patrilateral vs. Patrilineal.* The B's are ego's patri*lateral* kin (because he is related to them through his father), as are the A's. But the A's are his patri*lineal* kin, while the B's are not. The C's, and others on mother's side, are *matri*lateral.

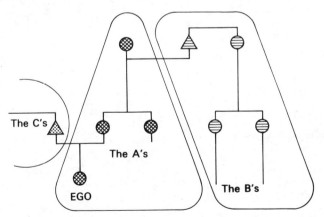

FIGURE 5   *Matrilateral vs. Matrilineal.* In a different society, where descent is traced matrilineally, the reverse pattern is found. Here the B's are ego's matri*lateral* kin, as are the A's. But the A's are her matri*lineal* kin, while the B's are not. The C's, and others on father's side, are *patri*lateral.

kin); and if we look at ego's mother's father's descent group in a matrilineal descent system (who are matrilateral but not matrilineal kin).

In all societies, then, kinship is culturally reckoned and socially important. In the tribal world, webs of kinship connect wider ranges of people, and shape their lives in more crucial ways, than in modern industrial societies. And in many of these tribal societies, descent has emerged as a highly adaptive solution to the special problems of forming viable groups, binding these groups together into an enduring political order, and relating humans to the land and other property on which life depends. To see how and why, we need to look more closely at descent systems and how they work.

3
PATRILINEAL DESCENT AND THE PERMUTATIONS OF DESCENT SYSTEMS

There are several reasons why it is useful to consider systems where patrilineal descent groups predominate before going on to look at societies where descent groups are formed matrilineally or cognatically, and then at more complex or specialized systems. This is an anthropologically traditional way of viewing descent—though one that has sexist overtones and can well raise feminist eyebrows or wrath. There are better reasons than tradition for this approach.

(1) First of all, patrilineal descent groupings are far more common than matrilineal (or cognatic) ones. Keeping in mind the dangers of classing a society as patrilineal or matrilineal, it is worth looking at some statistics (see Table 2 on the next page).

That patrilineal systems predominate statistically reflects first some ecological pressures. Predominantly pastoral societies, with a male-dominated division of labor and usually considerable mobility, are characteristically patrilineally organized (Aberle 1961; Rubel 1969; Pastner 1971). Even in predominantly agricultural or horticultural societies, patriliny very often prevails. Apparently matrilineal descent systems represent relatively specialized adaptations to ecological conditions favoring settlement in largish sedentary communities, and favoring a division of labor where crucial agricultural tasks are in the hands of women. We will return to these questions in Chapters 4 and 9.

TABLE 2

Frequency of Descent Rules (Based on Aberle 1961; derived from Murdock 1957.) (Originally published by the University of California Press; reprinted by permission of The Regents of the University of California.)

DESCENT TYPE	NUMBER OF CULTURES	%
Patrilineal	248	44
Matrilineal	84	15
Double and bilineal*	28	5
Bilateral and other	205	36
	565	100

* Includes Australian section systems; see Chapter 5.

2 Another set of reasons for using patrilineal systems as a point of departure and comparison is structural. For various ecological, biological, and organizational reasons we will examine in Chapter 6, matrilineal descent systems operate under severe constraints. Only certain fairly limited permutations of the possible forms of descent organization seem to produce viable forms. For this reason, patrilineal descent can at the outset serve to set out the range of organizational possibilities and define a conceptual tool kit. This theoretical equipment will then serve us well when we turn to consider the less common and more narrowly constrained forms of descent organization.

It is hard for students who live in Western industrialized societies, in urban settings, and whose closest social ties are to friends and neighbors, not relatives, to visualize social life in a tribal society—where the scale of community is drastically reduced, and where kinship and descent define where you live and how you relate to the people in your social world. It is useful to many to introduce unfamiliar modes of organizing social relations by phrasing them in more familiar terms: to describe a hypothetical descent system in terms with which the Western reader is familiar. Having viewed an idealized imaginary system in these terms, we will command a model against which to contrast the many variant forms found in the real world.

A HYPOTHETICAL PATRILINEAL DESCENT SYSTEM

Imagine a town of some 10 or 20 thousand people, composed of six districts. Each district is made up of some five or ten small neighborhoods (see Figures 6 and 7). All of the people in the town have one of a dozen names—Smith, Jones, Brown, and so on. (Readers who find these names too WASPish can substitute others. These have the advantage of being short, familiar, and pronounceable by English-speakers.) Children, as in our society, have the same last name as their father. No two people with the same last name are supposed to marry. town
district
neighborhood
street

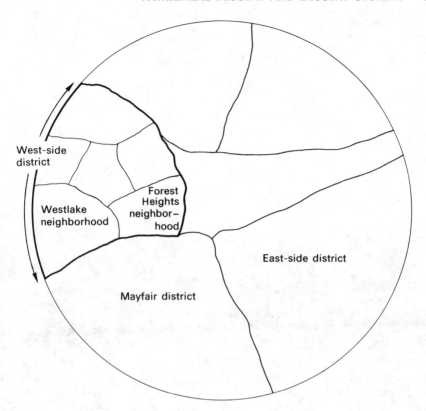

FIGURE 6   The Districts of our "Patrilineal Descent" Town, and the West-Side Neighborhoods.

In one specific *neighborhood*, the houses and land on a particular street are all owned by people with the same name. Let us narrow our focus to the Smiths living on Elm Street (Figure 8). All of them are descended from Sam Smith, the grandfather of the oldest men now living. The land where they live on Elm Street is owned by them collectively. Each Smith has a separate household for his family, though families assist one another in their work.

John Smith, one of the older men, acts as spokesman for these Elm Street Smiths in business and property matters, and leads them at religious services in the shrine at his house. One of the peculiarities of the legal system is that should one of the Elm Street Smiths get married, injure someone, or commit a crime, all of the Elm Street Smiths join together to bear the costs, or are all held accountable. To an outsider, one Elm Street Smith is as good as another. Note that it is only the Smith men, their wives (who are not Smiths), and their unmarried children who live on Elm Street. The married daughters of Smiths have gone to live with their husbands.

Westlake neighborhood

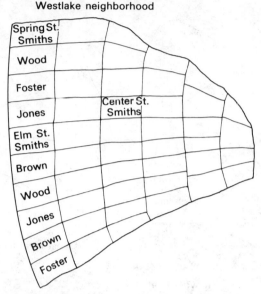

FIGURE 7   The Local Groups in Westlake Neighborhood.

On the next street lives a group of Joneses, and on the other side a group of Browns. But within this neighborhood there are six other streets of Smiths. All of these Smiths are descended from a common great-great-grandfather; and they recognize this common descent (from George Smith) at a neighborhood Smith church. There George Smith is buried, and there they occasionally gather for collective rites. The neighborhood Joneses, Browns, and others also have their own churches. The people with a common name and a common church own only church property collectively, and although they do a few nonreligious activities together, they are not a tight little group like the Elm Street Smiths.

All of the Smiths within the district seldom see one another, except at a yearly religious outing, but they have a general feeling of unity based on the common descent they trace from a Smith ancestor seven generations ago.

Finally all Smiths in the *town* believe that they are descended from a founding Smith, though they do not know how they are related. They have a few common religious symbols, but have no further social unity. Recall that ideally no two Smiths—however remotely related—are supposed to marry. In fact, Smiths from different districts occasionally do marry, despite some disapproval. But marriage between two Smiths in the same district is regarded as very wrong, and marriage between Smiths in the same neighborhood would be strictly prohibited.

In everyday circumstances the Smiths on Elm Street are a separate corporation, and deal with other Smiths (even those in the same neighborhood church) as they would with anyone else. But if the Elm Street Smiths

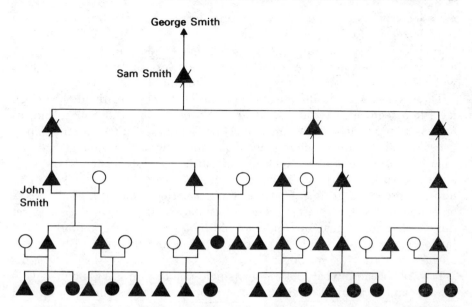

FIGURE 8   The Elm Street Smiths. The hypothetical genealogy shows the men, women, and children living on Elm Street. Note that most grown Smith women have married out, and non-Smith women have married in.

quarrel with Browns on a nearby street, or with another neighborhood, matters can escalate so that the Elm Street Smiths are joined by some or all Smiths of the neighborhood and the Browns are backed by other Browns. But such alliances, which may sometimes unite Smiths of the same *district* (but different neighborhoods), are temporary and limited to the particular dispute at hand. When things are settled—and this often comes from the arbitration of Smiths whose mothers are Browns and Browns whose mothers are Smiths—these alliances dissolve.

There are many variations on this pattern in the tribal world, and we will glimpse a few of them. First, some important features of patrilineal descent systems can be illustrated in terms of the Smiths and Joneses, and some needed technical terms defined.

First of all, note that the Elm Street Smiths are related by common descent; but so too are all the Smiths in the neighborhood, all the Smiths in the district, and—according to tradition—all the Smiths in town. That is, descent categories can be formed at higher and higher levels, with more and more remote "apical" ancestors serving as the point of reference. But note that the Elm Street Smiths form a *descent group*, while all the Smiths in town form only a *descent category*. The Smiths on Elm Street form a solid little local corporation, with collective property, collective legal responsibility, and so on. The Smiths in the neighborhood form a group too, but the things they do and own as a group are much less important. The more inclusive descent categories serve to define the limits of exogamy and provide the bases for political alliances.

Such descent groups and categories, based on descent from more and more remote ancestors, are called *segmentary* (Smith 1956). A part of a wider hypothetical genealogy of Smiths is illustrated in Figure 9.

These systems are called segmentary because they are divided at each level into segments (the descendants of Sam, Joe, and Ed Smith; and, as higher-order segments, the descendants of George and Fred Smith). Their genealogical structure is hierarchical. But this view of them one gets at any time is "frozen," like one frame of a movie film. To understand how such a system works, and how groups form and change, we must look at it in terms of processes in time. Consider the Elm Street Smiths, a group based on common descent from grandfather Sam Smith. If we visited Elm Street three generations later, Sam Smith would be a great-great grandfather, and far too many Smiths would be descended from him to live on Elm Street. So how can the system work?

It works because what looks at any single point in time as though it were a stable and permanent arrangement of people, territories, and genealogical connections is in fact only a temporary crystallization. Over longer periods new groups are forming; old ones are dying out. When we look three generations later, John Smith (who was *leader* of the Smiths before) may now be treated as the *founder* of the Elm Street Smiths, who now will include

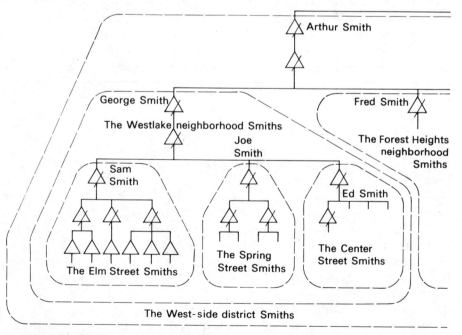

FIGURE 9   *The Genealogy of the Smith Lineages.*

his descendants but not those of the other men who lived with John Smith on Elm Street (see Figure 8). Some of John Smith's brothers and cousins may by this time have no living descendants; others may have had only daughters, or granddaughters, who have married and left. The descendants of others may have proliferated, but moved elsewhere to found new corporations, often because of internal quarrels or feuding. After the span of three generations, what had been a Jones street may now be a Smith street. All the Browns in the whole neighborhood may now have disappeared.

If we looked over a longer time span, descent groups would be seen as proliferating, dwindling, splitting off, disappearing, and by conquest, succession, or shifts of affiliation constantly changing their relationship to places. Nor do these rearrangements of peoples and places always follow the neat genealogical lines our first view had suggested. Anthropologists have found that more often it is the genealogical "charters" that are edited and rearranged to fit the realities of group structure and political relations at a given time. A segment of people who show up on the genealogies as Smiths may in fact be remnants of some other group allied with or protected by Smiths; and distantly "related" groups may not unite in feuding because they are Smiths, but may be Smiths because they unite in feuding.

At this stage, it will be useful to introduce several technical terms for talking about unilineal descent systems, and to illustrate further basic principles about how they work.

LINEAGES AND CLANS

A unilineal descent group whose members trace their descent from a known ancestor and know the genealogical connections to that ancestor, is technically called a *lineage*. In the case of the patrilineal Smiths and Joneses, we can call the descent groupings *patrilineages*; in a matrilineal system, they are called *matrilineages*. Note that lineages can occur at different hierarchical levels in a segmentary system: the Elm Street Smiths form a lineage, but so do the higher-level Westlake Neighborhood Smiths, and the still higher-level West-Side District Smiths. In segmentary systems, such "nested" lineages can be categorized as "maximal," "medial," and "minimal." Lineages are distinguished, however, from unilineal descent groupings whose members believe they are descended from a common ancestor, but do not know the genealogical connections. Such categories or groups are called *clans*. Thus, all the Smiths in our town form a patrilineal clan. When a society is conceived as divided into two parts, determined by descent, these are called *moieties* (patri-moieties if one belongs to one's father's side, matri-moieties if one belongs to one's mother's side). Finally, when several clans are allied into a single category, and there are three or more such clusters, the clusters are called *phratries* (sing. *phratry*).

SEGMENTARY SYSTEMS IN SPACE

The productive systems and ecology of tribal societies seldom permit the concentration of large populations of many thousands in towns. (Though there are some exceptions, especially in Africa. The Yakö of Nigeria actually have a town organization quite similar to the hypothetical town of Smiths and Joneses, though they have cross-cutting matriclans as well as patri-lineages; see Case 15.) More commonly, the tribal equivalent of our town is a region of many square miles, with "neighborhoods" scattered out over farmlands. Even the Elm Street Smiths might be scattered in homesteads, though often they would be clustered into a single hamlet or village. We will view some of these possibilities in the section on Kinship and Community (p. 39). But it will be well to remember at this stage that the texture of social relations in space is usually much more open than our hypothetical town would suggest.

There is an important axis of variation in segmentary patrilineal systems that we need to draw at this stage. In most such systems, it is only the lowest lineage level (minimal lineages) or lowest two levels that occupy single or contiguous territories and are thus localized. And usually it is only such localized segments (what Middleton and Tait [1958] call "nuclear groups" and Sahlins [1961] calls "residential proprietary segments") that are strongly corporate. Thus, in our hypothetical patrilineage system, the Smith lineages in Westlake District were scattered in between Browns and Joneses and Greens, not all lumped together. The higher-level, dispersed lineage segments (the Westlake Smiths, the West-Side District Smiths) are usually less strongly corporate (i.e., there are fewer contexts in which people act as a corporate unit, relative to fewer or less important things). At the highest level, descent units (especially at the level of clans or moieties) are not likely to be groups at all, but rather social categories that serve to define the outer limits of exogamy or minimal kinship obligation.

But there are a few societies where the geographical arrangement of territories corresponds neatly to the genealogical structure of lineage segments. In these systems, it is as though instead of Smith lineages being scattered around a neighborhood in which some streets are occupied by Joneses, and some by Browns, a whole neighborhood was made up of the descendants of George Smith (see Figure 9), and a whole district was made up of the descendants of Arthur Smith. There would be no Joneses and Browns mixed in (apart from in-marrying wives). The Tiv of Nigeria will serve to illustrate this mode of organization.

CASE 4: SEGMENTARY LINEAGES AMONG THE TIV

Among the Tiv of Nigeria the whole population of some 800,000 traces descent by traditional genealogical links from a single founding ancestor. Moreover, each level of the segmentary hierarchy corresponds to a separate territorial segment. It is as though instead of Smith lineages being scattered around a neighborhood also occupied by Joneses and Browns and others, a whole neighborhood was made up of Smiths, and an entire district was made up of Smiths, Browns, and Joneses, all of whom traced common descent from the same distant ancestor, and so on. Figure 10 illustrates this mode of segmentary organization among the Tiv.

Sahlins (1961) has urged that only this kind of system should be called "segmentary." He argues that such an organization is particularly adaptive when a tribe is expanding into another people's territory. The kind of alliances in warfare that such an arrangement makes possible would give the Tiv or Nuer (see Case 7) an advantage over their competitors, and hence would be adaptive for "predatory expansion."

LOCAL GROUPS AND DESCENT GROUPS

Another important feature of a system of unilineal descent groups is that for any particular corporation and its territory, there are two separate categories for membership. This can be clearly illustrated for the Elm Street Smiths.

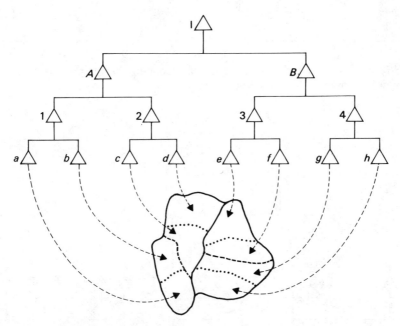

FIGURE 10   *Segmentary Organization among the Tiv.* Note here how the geographical distribution of lineages corresponds to their genealogical relationships. (From P. Bohannan 1954, by permission of the International African Institute.)

First, there are all those men, women, and children whose fathers were Elm Street Smiths, and hence are members of the corporation by birth. But not all of them live there. The adult Elm Street Smith women have mainly left to live with their husbands, and are scattered around other streets and neighborhoods. Second, there is the group of persons actually living on Elm Street: Smith men, their wives (who are not Smiths), and their children. The *descent group*, which is only partly localized, and the *local group*, which is only partly based on descent, are usually both important in different contexts—and it is dangerously easy to confuse them. The contrast is shown in Figures 11 and 12.

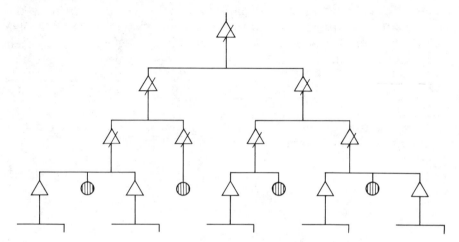

FIGURE 11   A Patrilineal Descent Group (descent group members who live elsewhere shown with vertical hatching).

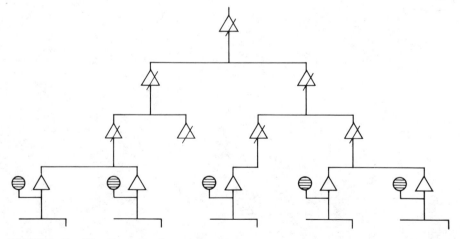

FIGURE 12   The Descent-Based Local Group (local group members who are not descent group members shown with horizontal hatching).

In a patrilineal system, the relative strength of ties between a woman and her husband, and between a woman and her brother, is always important. In some systems, a woman retains very strong ties to her (natal) lineage, and her father or brother retain strong legal rights over her. (The male chauvinism is that of the tribesmen.) In others, a woman's ties to the lineage of her birth are virtually severed, and she becomes strongly affiliated with her husband's lineage. Among the early Romans, this was carried to its extreme: when a girl was married, she was ushered ritually out of her family and the cult of her lineage ancestors, and into the family of her husband and father-in-law (she even acquired, by legal fiction, her husband's ancestors [Fustel de Coulanges 1864]). Her husband then exercised over her the same set of legal rights previously held by her father. We will see shortly how this pair of relationships between a woman and her brother and a woman and her husband, affects matrilineal systems.

Much confusion in the anthropology of social organization has resulted from a failure to keep straight the difference between a descent group, which does not include in-marrying spouses and which thus is not localized, and a descent-based local group, which includes in-marrying spouses but excludes out-marrying descent group members. Usually both are important. The trick is to find out in what contexts, and in what ways, and to keep from blurring them together as "the localized descent group" (see Keesing 1971).

DESCENT GROUPS AND DOMESTIC GROUPS

The core of the family, in comparative perspective, is the unit of mother-plus-dependent children (Goodenough 1970; cf. Goody 1972). When a *uterine family* father is joined to this unit, the result is a "nuclear" or conjugal family. But the roles a husband/father plays in our society—as mother's spouse, as mother's sexual partner (and begetter of children), as provider, as disciplinarian, as legal guardian—are not always assumed by mother's husband in non-Western societies. The mother's brother, for example, can assume all these roles but those of spouse and sexual partner. Among the Nayar castes of Malabar, in South India, the domestic group consists of a small cluster of brothers and sisters related matrilineally. The sisters bear children by lovers, who visit them; the brothers act as disciplinarians, guardians, and providers. The domestic group is a small corporation, a segment of a matrilineage.

The nuclear units of mother-plus-children may constitute independent units, as in the "matricentric" families of the Caribbean; or may be linked together, as in African polygynous societies where each co-wife and her children constitute a separate household. Viewing mother-and-children as forming a family nucleus enables us to fit into the comparative spectrum some of the arrangements that have grown out of women's liberation movements, particularly where sexual bonds between women and legal and economic independence have eliminated male performance of traditionally male roles.

Domestic groups can then be seen as building on the family core—by adding father, by stringing conjugal families together by a rule of descent, by linking several mother-child units to a single husband-father, and so on. This suggests the way that descent and family structure can be intertwined.

A domestic group may consist of two or more generations of patrilineally-related men, or matrilineally-related women, or even matrilineally-related men and their spouses. Each of the component nuclear family groups may comprise a partly separated household, with these subhouseholds linked together. Such a wider combined grouping has been traditionally called an "extended family" or "joint family." But notice that the line between such an "extended family" and a descent-based local group like the Smith families who live on Elm Street becomes fairly arbitrary. (One could adopt the convention that they are a "family" only if they live under the same roof, but that may be inappropriate where many families occupy a long-house [Borneo] or a huge hut [parts of Amazonia].) What has been called an "extended family" among the Tiv of Nigeria could just as well be called a lineage-based local group, as in Case 5.

CASE 5: PATRILINEAL EXTENDED FAMILIES AMONG THE TIV

Among the Tiv, the domestic unit of production is the compound group. The Tiv compound is an oval or circular arrangement of huts and granaries, with a central open space that is the "center of Tiv family life" (Bohannan and Bohannan 1968:15). The nucleus of the compound group is a senior man, the oldest in the group, who acts as its head. He arbitrates disputes, controls magical forces, and supervises production.

He has several wives, each of whom would normally have a separate hut in the compound. The compound group typically includes the head's minor children and unmarried daughters, and his married sons and their wives and children. To this extended family core may be added a younger brother of the head and his wives and children, or a nephew of the head. These may also be outsiders—friends or age-mates of the men at the compound—who live there. The membership of the compound group, especially among these others attached to the extended family core, may shift considerably over time. The genealogical composition and spatial arrangement of one Tiv compound are diagrammed in Figure 13.

While in a sense each wife who has a separate hut and her children constitute a separate domestic unit, the larger compound group—a

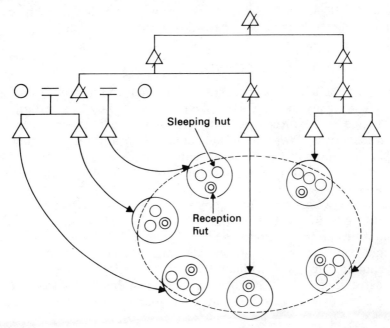

FIGURE 13   Map and Genealogy of a Tiv Compound. (After a diagram in
P. Bohannan, *Tiv Farm and Settlement* [Colonial Research Study No. 15, 1954],
by permission of the Controller of Her Britannic Majesty's Stationery Office.)

patrilineal extended family augmented by outsiders—is the central
domestic unit of everyday Tiv life and of collective economic enterprise (Bohannan and Bohannan 1968).

   The relationship of descent groupings to domestic groupings depends on
the rule(s) of *postmarital residence* in a particular society. A "residence
rule" specifies where a couple should live after marriage: *viri*locally (with
the husband's people) or *uxori*locally (with the wife's people); it is possible, of course, that they may be enjoined or permitted to live *neo*locally—
to establish a new and separate place of residence. Sometimes two or more
alternative modes of residence are culturally appropriate possibilities in
the same society, with the choice between them a matter of economic
strategy, personal circumstance, or the negotiations of the marriage contract.
   In most societies with patrilineal descent groups, a pattern of virilocal
residence prevails, as with the Smiths and Joneses, and the Tiv. This creates
the convergence between domestic groupings and descent-based local groups
illustrated for the Tiv. In societies with matrilineal descent, as we will see,
there are several possible residence patterns, each of which has crucial
structural implications. Finally, it is possible that even with patrilineal
descent corporations, a residence pattern may prevail that sets up cross-

cutting rather than congruent domestic groups. The Shavante of central Brazil are a rare well-documented case of this particular pattern.

CASE 6: SHAVANTE HOUSEHOLDS

The Shavante Indians of central Brazil are organized in corporate patri-lineages. Like many of the Gê-speaking peoples, they live in large cir-cular villages that express spatially the schemes of their cosmology (Lévi-Strauss 1963). Yet unlike their close cultural relatives, they can-not assign a sector of the circle to each lineage because patrilineally related men are scattered around the circle in their wives' parents' households.

At marriage, a Shavante man goes to live with his wife's parents. A household consists, at one stage in its cycle, of a couple and their children. The children belong to their father's patrilineage—yet their father had come at first as an outsider into the hostile setting of his in-laws' house. Now, as he himself is established, his sons marry and must leave the security of their household. The daughters stay, marry-ing before puberty and bringing in their young husbands as insecure outsiders.

Ideally men marry more than one wife, posing obvious problems. The best solution is to marry two sisters. In fact young men of the same patrilineage can help to stay together, despite marriage, if they marry girls who live next to one another. Strategic marriage of a cluster of patrilineally related men to a local cluster of closely related girls is an ideal solution that helps to keep the lineage together (Maybury-Lewis 1967).

It should also be remembered that even where the "rule of descent" and "rule of residence" correspond, they may not produce neat unilineal groups actually living together. Even where patrilineal descent is strongly empha-sized in ideology, local groups still may include an assortment of bilateral kin and affines as well as patrilineally related kin. An interesting and classic case, described by Evans-Pritchard (1940, 1951) and recently reanalyzed by Gough (1971) are the Nuer of the Sudan. Nuer local groups and their political relations are conceptualized in terms of segmentary patrilineal descent (see Case 7, below). But the actual composition of Nuer local groups is highly variable, with bilateral kin and affines attached to a lineage core or to a strong leader. "If a man is not a member of the lineage with which he lives, he makes himself a member of it by treating a maternal link as though it was a paternal one, or through affinal relationship" (Evans-Pritchard 1951:48). "The actual domestic relations of a large proportion of the [Nuer] population . . . do not fit the ideals of patrilineal descent, but are continually reinterpreted, through a series of customary legal fictions, so that the ideals are preserved" (Gough 1971:115).

KINSHIP AND COMMUNITY

The articulation of kin groups with local groups needs to be examined from another direction. As noted in the Preface, it is misleading to class together, on the basis of formal features, societies that differ greatly in scale and technology. This is nowhere more apparent than when we look at the communities—homesteads, hamlets, villages, towns, or even cities—where descent groups have their local base.

At one end of a continuum are small-scale societies such as those in much of Melanesia where descent groups consist of only, say, 20 to 50 members, and where they may well live in scattered homestead or homestead clusters. Toward the other end, there may be large towns of several thousand within which descent groups are arranged in wards or "barrios." In such diverse societies, descent groups may serve quite different adaptive ends.

This range can be expressed in terms of our Smiths and Joneses. In some unilineal descent systems, the equivalent of the Elm Street Smiths would be perhaps a half dozen or dozen men and their families; and "Elm Street" would be an area of several square miles through which the houses of Smith men are scattered or grouped in smaller clusters. The "neighboring" Joneses would be on the other side of the mountain; and the "West Side" would be a sparsely populated area of many square miles.

In other societies further along the continuum, "Elm Street" might be a closely grouped hamlet of 30 families or a village of 100 households. Finally, where technology or concentrated resources have permitted a greatly expanded, dense population, a town not unlike the one we set the Smiths and Joneses in at the outset may actually exist in the "primitive" world.

In addition to this range of variation in the size and spatial concentration of communities—from scattered homesteads to larger towns—there are formal features of the articulation of kin groups to communities that are worth setting out systematically. These relationships shape the nature of tribal social life and political relations in crucial ways.

These possible relations between communities and descent groupings have been usefully classified by Hogbin and Wedgewood (1953) in a survey of local groupings in Melanesia. Their scheme has not been widely used partly because it seems to be regionally bound (though it need not be); and because of a series of neologisms they attach to their types (e.g., "non-osculant multicarpellary parish") that have frightened away would-be borrowers. Using Smith and Joneses and schematic drawings, we can avoid these formidable labels while capturing the virtues of their analysis.

First, a corporate kin group may be coterminous with a separate community. That is, one local lineage or clan lives together in a village. More precisely, a descent-based local group (including in-marrying spouses but not out-marrying siblings) will be localized in a single community. In Figure 14, the Smiths thus constitute a separate village. Given a rule of descent group exogamy, spouses will have to come from surrounding villages, and bonds of intermarriage will tie villages together.

If one descent corporation comprises a separate community, then an important question is whether this lineage-village is related by common descent to other segments—whether there are other villages composed of Smith lineages. In some lineage systems, there are only local lineages; there are no segmentary descent relationships uniting a village group to others. The potential importance of this contrast in the political relations between villages is obvious. If the village-based lineage stands alone, its closest relationships will be to surrounding villages. Presumably these surrounding villages will be those with whom its members have intermarried. However, if members of our Smith lineage-village are related by common descent to other Smith lineages, these will give them outside political alliances (Figure 15). The outside world of a people is likely to be divided into non-Smiths, with whom one can marry, and fellow Smiths, who are potential allies.

Very commonly, however, there are several different descent groups in a single settlement (Figure 16). In such a society, if the lineages or clans are strongly corporate, they are likely to be separated into *wards* or "barrios"; each descent group has its own segment of the village. Note that this raises

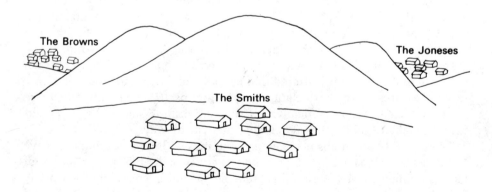

FIGURE 14 Type I. A community consists of members of a single descent group (and their spouses). There are no other Smith communities. Since each community descent group is exogamous, wives must come from neighboring communities; neighboring communities are thus bound together by strands of kinship and intermarriage.

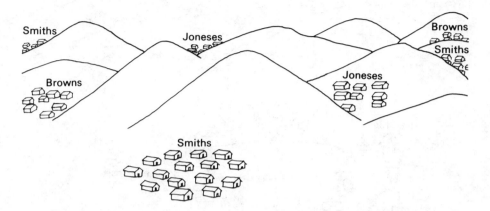

FIGURE 15 Type II. A community consists of members of a single descent group (and their spouses). Each local descent group is a segment of an overarching descent grouping that includes other villages. Thus a Smith community is related by common descent to other Smith communities; and by ties of intermarriage and kinship to surrounding Brown, Jones, and other communities.

the possibility that marriage can take place primarily within the village, among its two or more descent groups. In some societies there is a clear preference, or even requirement, for village *endogamy*, or "in-marriage." A man is supposed to marry the girl across the plaza, if not next door. One fascinating variant is an exogamous moiety system where each village is divided between the two moieties. The village in such a society may be laid out in a way that expresses the social and cosmological opposition of segments. The circular villages of the peoples of central Brazil are particularly spectacular examples.

Where a hamlet, village, or town includes several different descent groups, each may be related in segmentary fashion to descent groups in other communities (Figure 17). In terms of our example of the Smiths and Joneses, we can imagine such a situation in this way: a *village* corresponds to what we earlier called a "neighborhood." That is, the Elm Street Smiths and the surrounding Brown, Jones, and other local lineages live in separate segments of a town. Some miles away, in another town, live other lineages of Smiths, Browns, and Joneses. In such a system, the ties between lineages in the same village—the ties of *community*—may transcend in everyday affairs the ties of common descent linking dispersed descent groups in different villages. This underlines the fact that wherever several descent groups live in a single community, what they do collectively as villagers and townsfolk or simply as neighbors may be at least as important as what they do as members of separate corporations.

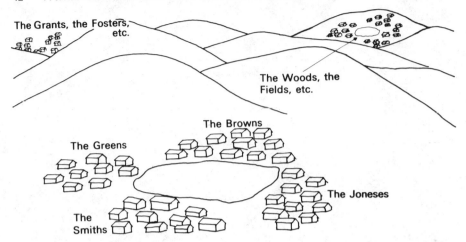

FIGURE 16   Type III. A community consists of several descent groups, often in somewhat separate wards. These have no other segments in other communities; and marriage is characteristically with other descent groups in the same community. Thus the community tends to be relatively autonomous from surrounding ones, and may have a strong unity that transcends descent group loyalties.

DESCENT GROUPS, MARRIAGE, AND AFFINITY

We have noted that descent groups are characteristically exogamous; that is, marriage within the lineage or clan is prohibited. In fact frequently, as with the Smiths and Joneses, marriage is prohibited not only within the corporate lineage, but at some more inclusive segmentary level as well. Often clans have little function other than defining the outer limits of exogamy.

We should make explicit what some theorists have overlooked: exogamy and the incest taboo are not the same thing. The incest taboo defines the limits of prohibited sexual relations; and violating it is very often unthinkable or a very severe offense. Exogamy defines the limits of socially-approved *marriage*. In a great many systems (including many segmentary systems, rigid class systems, etc.), there are girls or women a man can quite legitimately have intercourse with but could not legitimately marry (one can turn around this sexist phrasing, and say that girls can choose sexual partners who cannot be marriage partners).

Marriage in tribal societies is often misunderstood because Western observers begin with the wrong premises. In these societies marriage is characteristically a *contract between corporate groups*. Such a contract entails the transfer of a member of one corporation to residence with the other, and hence the loss of work services. Most often, it is the wife who leaves her descent group to live with her husband (though compare the matrilineal Hopi and Iroquois in Cases 11 and 12 below). Moreover, the corporate group that loses its member in marriage also gives up rights to the children of the marriage. It is best to think of this as a transfer of rights, over work services, reproductive powers, and so on. And since marriage is a contract, a transfer of these rights is usually balanced by material and symbolic recompense. When a lineage gives up its women in marriage it characteristically receives *bridewealth* (or bride price) in return. Such bridewealth may consist of money, ceremonial valuables, cattle, or other conspicuous goods.

Seeing marriage as a contract between corporate groups, not simply as a union of individuals, renders immediately intelligible customs that have often seemed strange to Western observers: the *levirate*, where upon the death of a husband his brother or other close relative marries his widow; and the *sororate*, where upon the death of a wife, the surviving husband marries her sister or other close kinswoman. In terms of a contract between corporations, it is clear what is happening. In the levirate the lineage that has acquired contractual rights over a woman is substituting a new husband for the deceased one, and maintaining the corporation's rights (especially to future children); in the sororate, the dead wife's lineage is providing a substitute and maintaining the contract.

In-laws are technically called *affines*, and their relationship is one of *affinity*. When one descent corporation enters into a marriage contract with another corporation, the wife's relatives become her husband's affines, and the husband's relatives become his wife's affines. To what extent this rela-

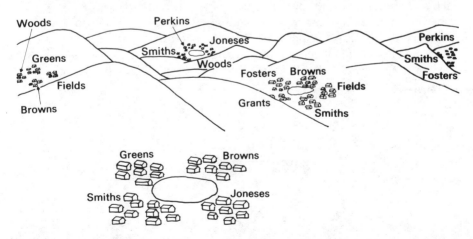

FIGURE 17 Type IV. A community consists of several descent groups. Some or all of the local descent groups are related by common descent to groups in neighboring communities. Hence they have external ties of kinship and local solidarity with their neighbors.

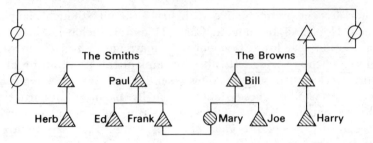

FIGURE 18   *Affines and Kin.*   Are Bill and Paul one another's in-laws? Are Ed and Joe one another's in-laws? Are Harry and Herb one another's in-laws or cousins? These are crucial questions in unravelling kinship and affinity in a unilineal descent system.

tionship of affinity is extended to the other members of the corporations vis-à-vis one another is an interesting (and often inadequately reported) axis of variation.

Imagine here that Frank Smith of the Elm Street Smiths has married Mary Brown of the nearby Olive Street Browns (Figure 18). The fathers of the bride and groom, Paul Smith and Bill Brown, may in such a system become one another's affines; but they may not. Note that in our system they are not in-laws to one another. But what about Frank's cousin Herb, on Elm Street, and Mary's cousin Harry, on Olive Street? Do they become affines to one another? They may already be kinsmen, because Herb's mother's mother was a sister of Harry's grandmother. Do they change their relationship just because Frank and Mary have gotten married? In most such systems, they would not. The marriage contract between two corporations does not usually make all members of one corporation affines of all members of the other (a point often overlooked in theoretical discussion).

Moreover, the affinal relationship changes in the next generation (Figure 19). Frank's brother Ed and Mary's brother Joe may be affines (or at least Ed is Mary's affine, and Joe is Frank's affine). But to Frank and Mary's

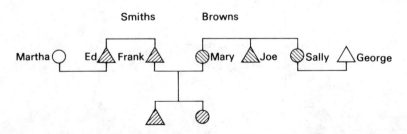

FIGURE 19   *The Next Generation.*   Joe and Sally are the children's aunt and uncle, not their in-laws; and so, in most unilineal systems (as in our own) are George and Martha.

children (who are Smiths), Mary's relatives (the Browns) are not affines; they are maternal uncles, aunts, and grandparents. For the children, as in our system, even Ed's wife Martha is an aunt, not an in-law; and Mary's sister Sally's husband is an uncle.

Thus, in such systems of contractual marriage between corporations, the relation of affinity seldom connects all members of one corporation with all members of the other. Moreover, it is a transitory relationship, that turns in the next generation into a relationship of kinship.

However, as we will see in Chapter 7, there are some systems where the affinal relationship between corporations is pervasive, stable, and enduring across generations. Such systems, known as *alliance* systems, were a focus of anthropological attention in the early 1960s.

Though descent groups in most tribal societies are exogamous, there are important exceptions. Among the Bedouin and some other Middle Eastern peoples, a system of agnatic lineages operates in conjunction with a marriage system that promotes lineage *endogamy*. The marriage system has been anthropologically described as "father's brother's daughter" (or "parallel cousin") marriage: a man ideally marries his *bint 'amm*, his father's brother's daughter; or alternatively, he may marry the daughter of his father's patri- lineally-related male cousin. It is more accurate to view this as a relationship between brothers, whereby a man has a *claim* on one of his brothers to provide a daughter for his son to marry. This custom has been interpreted by anthropologists as promoting lineage solidarity under conditions of desert hardship and pressure of warfare, or as preventing the dispersal of lineage wealth. It also reflects a sharp symbolic polarity between male and female, such that the children of two brothers or agnatic male cousins are con- trasted with the children of brother-and-sister (or cousins traced through a female link). Other observers have pointed out that in a system of lineage endogamy, kin will be related along multiple genealogical pathways due to the intermarriage of close relatives: a man and girl are likely to be related as the "right kind" of cousins by some path. In marrying, they give social recognition to their patrilineal connection, rather than alternative relationships.

The latter point is important. A largely endogamous local group may be conceptualized in terms of patrilineal descent (as with the Bedouin, but also on the Indonesian island of Bali and the Polynesian island of Tikopia), by according primary recognition to successive paternal links—even though both father and mother are likely to be from the same group. But alter- natively, as we will see in Chapter 6, in societies where many or most marriages take place within local groups, these groups may be conceptual- ized in terms of cognatic descent (the Maori, Case 19) or bilateral kinship (the Iban, Case 21).

The stability of marriage in tribal societies varies widely. In some, mar- riages are stable and enduring (though there is probably no other society that leads couples to expect that they should be "happy" in quite our sense). In others, marriage is highly unstable and divorces are very common. Theorists have for years argued about the correlates of stable and unstable marriage in tribal societies. It was noted some years ago that, for reasons we will see, marriage is characteristically unstable, and divorces common, in *matrilineal* descent systems (Richards 1950). But why are some patrilineal systems marked by stable marriage, others by frequent divorce? It had the makings of a great chicken-or-egg question. It was suggested by one theorist that it depended how "strong" patrilineal descent was. But it is hard to determine what "strong" means here; and this theory did not successfully sort out the low-divorce societies from the high-divorce societies. It was noticed that when divorce is relatively rare, bridewealth payments tend to be higher. But is this because a marriage is held together by the large transfer of valuables and the attendant difficulty of breaking the contract? Or can higher bridewealth feasibly be paid if marriages are relatively stable?

These questions, if not squarely answered, have at least been refined and pushed back a bit. For example, though marriage stability does not correlate neatly with the "strength" of patrilineality, it does correlate fairly neatly with the relative strength of two relationships: between brother-and-sister and between husband-and-wife. When a woman in a patrilineal system is cut largely adrift of membership or interests in her natal lineage (and hence her brothers have lesser control over her), then she is correspondingly more closely integrated into her husband's lineage, and tied to him with greater permanence. When her primary interests remain with the lineage of her birth, and her brothers have greater control over her despite her marriage, her bond to her husband and his lineage will tend to be fragile and impermanent. That at least leaves us with a smoother egg and a fatter chicken.

COMPLEMENTARY FILIATION AND COGNATIC DESCENT

In a unilineal descent system ties of kinship are always important. These are traced through the mother, in a patrilineal descent system, as well as the father (and through father as well as mother in a matrilineal system). Characteristically, in patrilineal systems, a young man has special and close ties to the mother's brother and other relatives (and secondarily, to father's maternal relatives and mother's maternal relatives).

In the early days of speculative historical reconstructions, this had often been viewed as evidence that societies had once been matrilineal. However, Fortes (1953, 1969) and Goody (1959, 1969)—following the lead of Radcliffe-Brown (1924)—showed that the importance of maternal kin was a normal element of the complex of patrilineal descent. Fortes called the ties to the mother's relatives and kin group *complementary filiation*. Such ties of filiation (i.e., bilateral kinship) complementary to the line of descent are important in at least some matrilineal descent systems, such as the Trobrianders (Case 13) (Robinson 1962).

"Complementary filiation" classes together both relations of interpersonal kinship with mother's brother and other kin and rights and ritual interests in mother's patrilineal *corporation*, father's mother's corporation, and mother's mother's corporation. As I have suggested for the Tallensi (Keesing 1970) and by implication for some other systems, there may be two separate principles confounded under the term "complementary filiation": on the one hand, ties of bilateral kinship; and on the other hand, a secondary principle of *cognatic descent*. Recall the illustration in Chapter 2 (page 22), that a Tallensi father could interact with his son both on the basis of kinship (as "father") and on the basis of descent (as "co-descendants of lineage ancestors"). The same apparently is true of a Tallensi maternal uncle, who can act toward his nephew both as a close and supportive kinsman and as a representative and fellow member of a lineage in which he has primary rights and his nephew has secondary rights due to cognatic descent. Thus the nephew, for example, has the right to partake of sacrifices to lineage ancestors, along with primary members. Recall that where a principle of cognatic descent is recognized, *all* of the descendants of an ancestor, whether through male or female links or through any combination of the two, are included as cognatic descendants. In a patrilineal descent system, the superimposition of a patrilineal descent category on a cognatic descent category leaves a residual category of nonagnates ("agnate" is another term for "patrilineal descendant"), descendants through one or more female links. In a matrilineal descent system there would be a similar residual category. It is convenient to group these negatively defined forms as *nonunilineal descent*[1] (see Figure 20) (Keesing 1968a).

A secondary principle of cognatic descent, that entitles nonunilineal descendants to secondary ritual interests, property rights, rights of residence, or "nonvoting" corporation membership, may in fact be operating in many societies where these secondary interests have been viewed as an expression of complementary filiation. Such secondary interests can operate, as in many highland New Guinea societies (see the Chimbu, Case 10 for an example, below), to redistribute population according to demographic changes, ecological pressures, and the shifting tides of feuding and warfare. A man can retain his *entitlement* to primary corporation membership in his patrilineal group, but opt to live with some other group to which he is related by cognatic descent, thus activating and strengthening his secondary rights.

---

[1] "Nonunilineal descent" had been used by some earlier writers (e.g. Davenport 1959) to designate what I am calling "cognatic descent." But since cognatic descendants include those who happen to be related either through all-male or all-female links (and hence are "unilineal"), the negative label is inappropriate (see Scheffler 1966, Keesing 1968a).

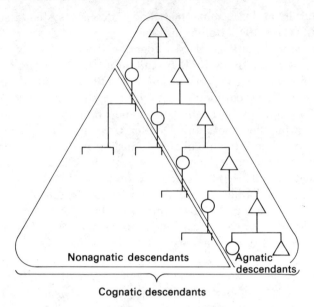

Nonagnatic descendants   Agnatic descendants

Cognatic descendants

FIGURE 20   *Unilineal, Nonunilineal, and Cognatic Descent.* The agnatic or patrilineal form is shown; the matrilineal version would be its mirror image (i.e., with sexes reversed).

In terms of the Smiths and Joneses, if some pressure of internal quarreling, land shortage, or the like made it undesirable for Larry Smith to live with the members of his Elm Street Smith corporation, he could go and live with the Maple Street Browns, his mother's people, or with the Laurel Street Joneses, his father's mother's people, on the basis of his cognatic descent from their founding ancestors.

In many patrilineal descent systems, marriage within the mother's lineage or clan is prohibited (as well as marriage within the father's). This is the case, for example, among the Chimbu of New Guinea (Case 10). There, marriage is forbidden within the father's clan and within the mother's subclan (though not in other subclans of the maternal clan). The effect of such "matrilateral exogamy" is to limit repeated marriages between the same local corporations—hence, to widen the range of affinal and cognatic kinship ties.

DESCENT SYSTEMS AND THE POLITICS OF TRIBES WITHOUT RULERS

The way Smiths and Joneses unite in temporary alliances larger than the local segments (the Elm Street Smiths) in feuds and disputes is central to the political organization of "tribes without rulers," (Middleton and Tait

1958). Such societies have been a focus of social anthropology in Africa. In many African patrilineage systems, there is no overarching governmental structure, no hierarchy of authority above the level of local lineages. Warfare and feuding can easily escalate in such a system, where every lineage is potentially opposed to every other. Alliances at higher segmentary levels are temporary and fragile (and they are always alliances "against," not alliances "for").

The preservation of honor often demands vengeance when people would rather live in peace. But there are, in such a system, always some people whose kinship obligations lead them quite legitimately to pour oil on the troubled waters (Smiths whose mothers are Browns, Browns whose mothers are Smiths . . .). Research by Max Gluckman and his students on segmentary lineage systems in Africa has emphasized the positive and equilibrium-maintaining function of conflict: resolution of feuds and warfare on the basis of cross-cutting ties of kinship is a reaffirmation of the moral bonds that hold the society together, in contrast to the cleavages of descent that separate tribesmen into opposing groups. The operation of such a system among the Nuer of the Sudan provides a good illustration.

CASE 7: NUER SEGMENTARY ORGANIZATION

Some 200,000 Nuer live scattered across the swamplands and savanna of the Sudan. Though there is no overarching government, the Nuer maintain a measure of unity and orderly political relations between the territorial divisions Evans-Pritchard (1940) calls "tribes," and between segments of them.

A Nuer tribe is the largest group whose members are duty bound to combine in raiding and defense. Each tribe has a territory, a name, and bonds of common sentiment. Within a tribe, feuds are supposed to be controlled by arbitration.

A tribe is divided into segments. The relationship between segments is conceived in terms of hierarchies of patrilineal descent, as with the Smiths and Joneses—even though the actual correspondence between descent and the composition of territorial groups is quite messy. The basic principle is contextual opposition and alliance: "We fight against the Rengyan, but when either of us is fighting with a third party we combine with them" (Evans-Pritchard 1940:143). In Figure 21, "when segment Z^1 fights Z^2, no other section is involved. When Z^1 fights Y^1, Z^1 and Z^2 unite as Y^2. When Y^1 fights X^1, Y^1 and Y^2 unite, and so do X^1 and X^2. When X^1 fights A, X^1, X^2, Y^1, and Y^2 all unite as B. When A raids the Dinka (a neighboring people), A and B may unite" (Evans-Pritchard 1940:143–144).

Disputes begin over many grievances—cattle, damage to property, adultery, or rights over resources, to name a few. The Nuer are prone

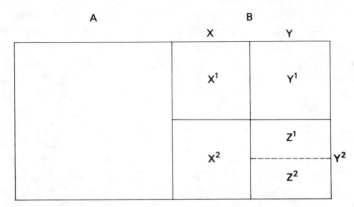

FIGURE 21   Nuer Political Organization.   A and B are the major segments of a Nuer "tribe" (Evans-Pritchard 1940). X and Y are the major branches of B, and they are in turn divided by segmentation. (From Evans-Pritchard 1940, by permission of The Clarendon Press, Oxford.)

to fighting, and many disputes lead to bloodshed. Within the same village, Nuer fight with clubs or without weapons. Confrontations between members of different villages can lead to use of spears and to bloody war between men of each village. When a man has been killed, the dead man's close patrilineal kin will try to kill the slayer or one of his close patrilineal kin. The slayer goes to a "Leopard-skin chief" for sanctuary; the latter seeks to mediate and to get the aggrieved lineage to accept "blood-cattle" and thus prevent a blood feud. A killing involving members of low-level segments who thus have close social relationships, like Z^1 and Z^2 or even Z^1 and Y^1, is likely to be settled without blood vengeance. The more distantly related the groups involved are, the greater the probability of large-scale fighting between temporary alliances like the X's versus the Y's.

But what about the Leopard-skin chief who arbitrates disputes and provides sanctuary? Does this not indicate some overarching political organization? According to Evans-Pritchard (1940), such a "chief" has ritual powers and a role as mediator and negotiator; but he has no secular authority, no special privileges. His performance in peacemaking is possible because he stands outside the lineage and tribal system, not because he is central in it. He serves an important function which in other segmentary societies must usually be served by persons with conflicting obligations due to cognatic kinship ties that crosscut lineages. His presence enables Nuer to carry the posturing of hostility and threat further than they otherwise could, because he stands in the way of the actual killings most Nuer hope to avoid.

The Nuer political system is interesting in that changing perspectives on how it works and how it can be understood, in the years since Evans-

Pritchard's classic 1940 book *The Nuer*, reveal widening horizons in the study of social organization.

Evans-Pritchard's view of the Nuer was essentially static: his models show how Nuer society "works" in an ahistorical vacuum where equilibrium prevails. But more recently, studies by Newcomer (1972), Haight (1972), Gough (1971), and others have reexamined the Nuer more closely in temporal and ecological context. "Nuer society" emerges as an unstable stage in a process of invasion and assimilation of their cultural cousins, the Dinka, that was arrested and "frozen" by colonialism.

For our purposes, it suffices to suggest this change of view by sketching in barest outline a recent exchange between Greuel (1971) and Haight (1972) regarding the allegedly "powerless" Leopard-skin chief or mediator. Greuel suggested that far from being powerless, the Leopard-skin chief was (partly because of the cattle received for his services as mediator) a wealthy leader who could mobilize the support of a substantial coalition of followers. If a man murdered a close lineage kinsman, his relatives would offer blood-money; if he murdered a distant outsider, a blood feud was no threat to community solidarity. But if a man killed a marginally close kinsman or neighbor, where a blood feud would be disruptive of economic and social solidarity, the Leopard-skin chief could often effectively mediate. But he could do so because he could mobilize a dominant coalition with an interest in avoiding internal feuding. Thus, while he had literally no direct power to enforce decisions, he commanded much implicit political power.

Haight, invoking a historical interpretation, questions whether the Leopard-skin chief, who emerged to prominence (through personal ability) from a particular Leopard-skin lineage, usually was the center of a numerically dominant coalition. In many or most areas, the Leopard-skin lineage was not the dominant lineage; and Haight sees the power of the Leopard-skin chief in these areas as more religious than political. Where in some areas the Leopard-skin lineage exercised political dominance, the Leopard-skin chief might indeed mobilize support of a dominant coalition. But both situations, Haight argues (1972), are best understood in terms of the historical process of conquest whereby the Nuer maintained dominance over the Dinka by absorption, and preserved an egalitarian social order while keeping a firm hold on territories (see also Newcomer 1972 and Glickman 1972).

DESCENT, RULERS, AND RANKS

So far we have been dealing with the relatively simple situation where patrilineages are all of equal rank, pieces in a larger design that are each structurally equivalent. And we have been dealing with systems without hierarchical, centralized institutions of government. But lineage systems also occur in more complex patterns of ranking and hierarchy.

The development in Africa of institutions of kingship has led to a number of complex hierarchical patterns. Many African societies have royal or aristocratic lineages, in addition to commoner lineages. In a class-stratified society, even without a strong central ruler, unilineal descent groupings may structure social life within the layers of the social layer-cake, though not between them. The Bunyoro of Uganda illustrate one of many variations on this theme of hierarchy.

CASE 8: THE BUNYORO LINEAGE SYSTEM AND KINGSHIP

The Kingdom of the Nyoro of Uganda, who number about 100,000, is believed to comprise three historically separate ethnic groups: an original agricultural people; a pastoral invading group, the Huma; and a more recently invading Nilotic group, the Bito, from whom the Kings of modern times trace descent. Although the Nyoro have been much changed by colonial domination, the general outlines of the traditional system can be reconstructed.

The local groupings of traditional Nyoro society were (at least ideally) segments of patrilineal clans. A cluster of extended family households comprised a dispersed community. Just how these local lineages or clan segments were grouped territorially is difficult to reconstruct, since clans are now intermingled. But rituals, marriage transactions, the legal system, and the kinship terminology suggest that patrilineal descent groups may have been more strongly corporate in the past than in the historic period.

On top of this descent system, which fits roughly into the Smiths and Joneses pattern, was a system of kingship and political hegemony that resembled in some ways the feudal system of medieval Europe. At its apex was the King, descended from the traditional dynasty of Bito Kings. He exercised formal sovereignty over the entire society and land, expressed both in political authority and in sacredness. His health and well-being were critical for the well-being of his people; if he sickened, the entire country suffered.

Authority to administer territories was delegated by the King to chiefs: great chiefs controlled vast territories; lesser chiefs controlled local areas. But chieftainship at all levels was an appointed, not hereditary power; though it tended to be passed down in families, it could be withdrawn at the King's pleasure. Chieftainships were not strictly ranked, but varied in importance according to the size, population, and wealth of the territory controlled, and the closeness of relationship to the King. While the most powerful chiefs were members of the ruling

Bito dynasty, most lesser chiefs were Huma cattle-herders or peoples of the commoner group, descendants of men who had attracted the favor of a previous King.

The greatest chiefs, mainly Bito relatives of the King, were the "princes" of an aristocracy that commanded deference from commoners and lived from the surplus goods exacted as tribute from these common people. But these great chiefs were potential threats to the King's power, through rebellion and political struggles over succession. Their power was checked by their residence not in the territories they ruled over, but in the King's capital; each left the usual affairs of his area in the hands of a deputy. They thus served as links between the King, in whose court they were key figures, and the rural populations that provided foodstuffs, valuables, cattle, and warriors for the King.

Because the King represented, symbolized, and ruled the entire country, it was important that he not be involved with the interests of the Bito. The eldest son of the previous King traditionally held an office as Okwini, the King's "official brother"; and he had primary authority over affairs of the Bito ruling group. A half-sister of the King served as Kalyota, the King's "official sister." She in turn was officially in charge of the aristocratic Bito women, who enjoyed a high rank and prestige and were considered to be "like men," in contrast to commoner women with their domestic duties. Formerly, these women of rank were not allowed to marry or have children. The Kalyota's power was in fact considerable: she held estates like male chiefs, deriving revenue and services from them, and she settled disputes among the Bito women.

Thus, among the Nyoro a patrilineal descent system provided the basic corporate groups and shaped organization at a local level. Yet superimposed on this descent system was a feudal hierarchy, a hereditary aristocracy, and a King with sweeping political power and great sacredness (Beattie 1958, 1960).

The lineage systems illustrated in previous sections were simple in a second sense. That is, they occurred in relatively homogeneous populations, where one language and a common culture prevailed. But lineages are also found in complex societies that are historical conglomerates or composites, as with conquest states. This occurs in some parts of Africa, as with the Bunyoro and with the dominant Tutsi and numerically preponderant Hutu who since independence have been engaged in genocidal struggles. It also occurred in the Americas (e.g., the Inca state), in Southeast Asia, and in parts of India where endogamous castes may be made up of lineages. Thus not only social classes but ethnic groups or castes may be pieced together into larger systems, the component layers or units of which are unilineally organized. Where such hierarchy or heterarchy prevails, the wider system is characteristically not held together by ties of intermarriage and kinship. The component "pieces" are usually endogamous; hence unilineal descent cannot integrate them into a unified structure.

However, there are in some parts of the world societies where lineages are ranked according to the seniority of a line of descent, where descent at once stratifies and links together. The most extensive development of this pattern was worked out in Polynesia, in the Pacific. The ramifying ranking system of Tonga will serve to illustrate.

CASE 9: TONGAN SOCIAL STRUCTURE

The Tongan Islands had an aboriginal population of some 25,000. They were grouped into territorial units conceptualized as the lands of large patrilineages. The 13 major lineages (*ha'a*) of modern times trace descent through ancient ancestors. They in turn are segmented into smaller lineages at several levels of segmentation (though the labels for these lower-level lineages seem not to have been consistently applied).

Tongan society is pervaded by the principle of ranking. Within the extended family household, the senior man is classed as *ulumotua* (ancestor). He is succeeded by his younger brother or oldest child (the latter resulting, in some cases, in the *ulumotua* being a woman). Seniority here was determined by a Polynesian principle that rank passed directly down a line of first-born sons (or sometimes, daughters). Younger brothers and their descendants have a lower rank.

This principle of seniority, through primogeniture (ideally in the male line), was the basis of the elaborate ranking and stratification in the Tongan lineage system. Each descent group, at every segmentary level, had as its nucleus one or more chiefs (*eike*) and a cluster of "chiefs' attendants" (*matapule*). The other lineage members were commoners (*tua*).

The highest ranking chief in all of Tonga was the Tui Tonga, or paramount chief. In recent centuries, his role had become religious; he was the focal point of sacredness, due to his direct descent from ancient ancestors and ultimately the gods. Two other paramount chiefs, the Tui Haa Takalaua and Tui Kanokupolu, represented both great sacredness and broad secular power. They functioned as "national," rather than lineage, leaders.

The chiefs of lineages varied in power and sacredness according to the seniority of their descent. Lesser chiefs headed junior lineages and lower-order segments. Chiefs at all levels commanded deference and exercised a powerful and often arbitrary authority over commoners. Tribute was exacted, taboos were levied. Food surpluses were channeled upward through the status hierarchy, and then downward again to be consumed as reinforcements of the prestige, power, and largesse of the chiefs. So powerful were the great chiefs that they could arbitrarily exact property or life itself from their subjects at will (Gifford 1929). (Sahlins (1958) gives a summary of older sources; and Kaeppler (1971) gives a somewhat revised and newer picture.)

According to the ideal Polynesian blueprint, each lineage would be ranked according to the closeness of its apical ancestor to the senior line of descent: all members of a senior lineage would be senior to all members of a junior lineage. In practice, in Tonga as elsewhere in Polynesia, the senior members of a junior lineage are more highly ranked than the commoners of a senior lineage (Sahlins 1958:142–144). Moreover, lineages were shaped, and their power defined, not simply by genealogical status, but by the shifting tides of politics and warfare. The system was undoubtedly far more flexible in practice than it was in theory. Success in warfare or power politics would be reflected in rearrangements of the genealogies. Lineages were forming, hiving off, dying out. Tongan lineages were not exogamous (marriage was forbidden only with close bilateral kin). Marriage within the lineage, and the possibility of claiming higher descent status through the mother's side, created further flexibility. (Among the Maori, Case 19, the Polynesian possibility of tracing descent through the mother's father was carried considerably further.)

Among the Tongans, and in the Society Islands, Marquesas, Hawaii, and some other Polynesian groups, the combination of patrilineal descent with a ranking of ramified descent lines produced a flexible and effective political system controlled by powerful aristocrats.

At this point it is useful to remember again that descent systems do not occur in an ecological vacuum. They are adaptive solutions to the organizational problems posed by environments and means of production. (That is not all they are: ideological and historical forces, as with the spread of kingship and the formation of conquest states, clearly also shape social organization.) The ramified, ranked descent systems of Polynesia, Sahlins (1958) has suggested, represent in part an adaptive solution to patterns of resource distribution on some of the Polynesian islands. Contrasting these ramified lineage systems with those in Polynesia where local descent groups do not trace ties of descent at higher segmentary levels, Sahlins argued that the two developed in different environments. Where on an island there is little environmental diversity, and each territorial group got a "slice" of all the available resources (e.g., of the beach and lowlands and the mountains behind), it would be relatively self-contained economically; and ties of descent to outside lineages would not be necessary to create lines of trade and redistribution of specialized resources. But where the environment and its resources were diverse and specialized, local territorial groups would not be self-sufficient. The ramified descent lines and high-ranking lineages would provide a mechanism for redistributing resources. Tribute to the high-rank-ing chiefs, in the form of specialized resources, would flow up the branches of the lineage system; and they would be redistributed through the lineage network so as to make the special resources of one region available else-where. Lineage connections would also provide channels for trade and exchange of locally specialized resources. This ingenious argument has been rather harshly judged by Polynesian specialists, and Polynesian lineage systems can no longer be simply classified into one type or the other. But this ecological interpretation still serves as a useful illustration of the way complex social forms can serve adaptive ends; and thus of how we go astray if we simply class descent systems typologically on the basis of formal features. Descent systems are means of organizing effective social groups; and they must be effective in adapting to the challenges of an environment, competing with neighboring peoples, and maintaining order and produc-tivity across generations.

DESCENT, PATRIFILIATION, AND FLEXIBILITY

We have noted that there is a recurrent problem of adaptation in lineage systems to the fluctuation of resources and especially to the whims of demography. If the relationship of lineage segments to territories is rela-tively fixed and stable, then the normal fluctuations of demography quickly generate a problem. As noted in Chapter 2, one segment will have many male descendants, and will expand; another segment will have few descend-ants, or many females, and its population will contract. To some extent, this problem is managed in such systems by fission and fusion, with con-tinuing readjustment of the territories and periodic emendation of the genealogies. That is, a lineage that proliferates moves into and takes over territory of one that dwindles; or it displaces them by overt warfare. The displaced remnant group may disperse among other kin or may attach them-selves to another segment (so that the "evicted" High Street Smith group might attach themselves to the Elm Street Smiths for land and protection, or to unrelated political allies). Such a group of "refugee" Smiths who attached themselves to the Forest Street Browns might well show up as Browns on a genealogy after two or three generations. Such processes of fusion and fission, expansion and contraction, and constant flux have turned up very vividly in the highlands of New Guinea, where in some regions warfare has continued up until the last few years. Anthropologists perhaps have been misled by the seeming stability of lineage systems in the colonial areas where they have usually studied: the colonial powers may have imposed stability where before there had been flux.

But another process of adjustment has turned up dramatically in New Guinea highlands societies, a process that also seems to have been occurring in societies such as the Nuer where it was paid insufficient attention (Gough 1971). There can be a big gulf between descent entitlement and actual residence. In a society where segments are conceived as related along patrilineal lines, and where local ideology emphasizes that a person belongs to his father's group, a large percentage of men may in fact live and garden in a territory where they are not patrilineally related. A man is *entitled to* rights in his patrilineal territory; and he may maintain some interests and ritual ties there. But he actually lives with his mother's people, or his father's mother's people, or his mother's mother's people. In some New Guinea societies seemingly conceptualized along patrilineal lines, such as Bena Bena (Langness 1964), over half of the adult men are living in territories to which they are not patrilineally related. The Chimbu provide a good illustration of a more usual New Guinea highland situation.

CASE 10: THE CHIMBU OF NEW GUINEA

An anthropologist first looking at the Chimbu would be tempted to produce an all-embracing model of a segmentary patrilineage system, akin to that of the Smiths and Joneses.

The Chimbu, some 60,000 New Guinea people scattered through highland valleys and slopes are grouped into tribes: territorial groups of several hundred to several thousand people. These tribes are confederations of clans, whose lands are scattered in blocks through the tribal territories. Clans are conceived as patrilineally descended from a founder, and clusters of clans may be conceived as related as brothers (though genealogical ties between them are not known). The Chimbu clan is an exogamous patrilineal descent grouping, segmented into named subclans. Again, subclans are conceived as the descendants of a set of brothers, the sons of the clan founder. A clan varies in size from under 150 to over 1000, with an average of 600 to 700; a subclan ranges in size from 50 to 250. A clan usually has a main block of territory with some outlying blocks; a subclan similarly usually has a main territorial area within that of the clan, with some outlying tracts. Within the subclan, localized sections are classed as "one blood." These sections have patrilineal genealogies, and include some 12 to 40 men and their families. The men of "one blood" live in a single men's house. Their wives and children live in households scattered through the garden lands.

What we would seem to have here is a "classic" segmentary patrilineage system of the sort familiar from Africa. But it is worth taking a closer look. First of all, the segmentary structure of tribes and clans and subclans is not as neat as it appears at first glance. Chimbu are very much unconcerned with genealogical relationships—in fact, singularly disinterested in the past at all. Their way of talking about two segments as though their relationship were as father and son or brother and brother is more metaphorical than "patrilineal." A composite "correct" blueprint of the segmentary system put together by an anthropologist hides the fact that different groups and even different individuals within a group have widely divergent conceptions of what segments there are and how they fit together.

Moreover, if we actually count heads within a local group, we find that there are a number of men who do not appear on the patrilineal genealogy, but who act fully as members of the group. Some turn out to be the sons or grandsons of women members who brought their children home at divorce or lived uxorilocally with their husbands. Some are men living uxorilocally, living with cognatic kin for protection, and so on—a diverse lot. Similarly, some of the "one blood" agnatic members are nowhere to be seen—they are off living somewhere else, with maternal kin or father's maternal kin, affines, or others. About 80 percent of a subclan's resident men are agnates (patrilineally related members); about 10 percent are cognatically related, the descendants of female agnates; and 10 percent are affines or other miscellaneous temporary residents *domiciled* somewhere else. (For many New Guinea highlands peoples, the percentages of nonagnates are considerably higher.) Adoption and fosterage further scrambled residential alignments.

Before peace was imposed by the colonial regime, conquest and feuding continually rearranged tribal boundaries and set groups adrift to find refuge with kin or affines. Moreover, this was a society that set great store on individual networks of friendship, strategic investment, and partnership; so that individual choice and entrepreneurship, not collective action by corporate descent groups, was the dominant theme in Chimbu social life (Brown 1962, 1967, 1972; Brookfield and Brown 1963).

Whether these New Guinea highlands societies can best be viewed in terms of segmentary patrilineal descent has been much debated. Barnes (1962) questioned the use of "African Models in the New Guinea Highlands," pointing out that in many respects the Chimbu and their cultural relatives were different from the Tiv, Nuer, Tallensi, and other Africans: genealogical reckoning was shallow, nonagnates were easily incorporated into groups, segmentary processes and the ways of conceptualizing them seemed different. Barnes suggested that group membership in such societies depended not on patrilineal descent but on "cumulative patrifiliation." That is, you normally joined your father's group. But if due to circumstances you affiliated with your mother's or paternal grandmother's group, your children's rights in that group would be secure. For they, though not related by patrilineal descent, were related by patrifiliation to the group you had attached yourself to. Descent ideologies may be used at higher "segmentary" levels to conceptualize the relationship between larger segments. But often, in the New Guinea highlands, related segments are thought of as "brothers," with the genealogical connection between them unknown or unimportant (Strathern 1968). The distinction is a fine one, but it has received support from recent studies by Andrew Strathern (1972).

This is a useful reminder of the dangers of typologically equating the social organizations in one region with those of another. But it has also been useful, in the light of the New Guinea evidence, to reexamine searchingly what really happened in African lineage systems before colonialism froze their dynamics; and to ask whether the flux and flexibility, the gulf between ideological blueprint and who actually lives where, may have been greater than the classic African studies suggest (see Gough 1971).

The recent reinterpretations of the Nuer (Case 7) in terms of historical migration and conquest enable us to go a bit further. Even the notion of "a society" and its internal dynamics imposes too narrow a view. Anthropologists, studying the colonially-frozen mosaic of tribal societies and projecting it back into a timeless past, have assumed too often that the different "cultures" have been distinct entities for many centuries. But invasion, migration, assimilation—the appearance and disappearance of what we call "cultures"—have been continuing processes.

DESCENT GROUPS AS RELIGIOUS CULTS

Descent groups are very often, though not always, religious congregations as well as secular corporations. In much of tribal Africa, the Pacific, Asia, and elsewhere, religion centers around "ancestor worship" (Fortes 1960). That is, lineage ancestors are a spiritual focus of the group. Often they are propitiated by sacrifice. Shared sacredness as a ritual community is often as important a force for descent group unity as secular interests of the corporation in property and politics. In a segmentary system, sacrifices or other religious activities may bring together the lower-level lineages that normally act separately. Thus a ritual observance for apical ancestor Arthur Smith might temporarily unite all West-Side District Smiths in shared sacredness.

When anthropologists think of the living lineage members as "really there" and the ancestors as hypothetical figures on genealogies, they may be misunderstanding the way lineage systems look to the people who live in them. To a lineage member sacrificing to his ancestors, the ancestors are as much "really there" and ever-present as his next-door neighbors. The lineage, in a sense, is a single community of living and dead members; and communications and transactions between living and dead are a central part of lineage life (Kopytoff 1971).

Where sacrifice to descent-group ancestors brings the members of a lineage or clan together in shared sacredness and religious commitment, it is important to look carefully at the role of nonmembers—particularly of children and grandchildren of lineage members who have married out (the descendants of out-marrying women in a patrilineage system, or of out-marrying men in a matrilineage system). Among the Tallensi, as we have noted (Case 3), descendants of patrilineage women are entitled to partake of sacrifices to lineage ancestors. Men in patrilineage systems may raise animals for sacrifice to their maternal as well as patrilineal ancestors.

The nature of ancestral cults in unilineal descent systems poses fascinating problems. In the majority of African systems of ancestor worship, and a great many of those in Melanesia, South Asia, and elsewhere, ancestral spirits are punitive in their relationship to the living. A kindly old grandfather dies and, as a spirit, begins to visit sickness and death on his descendants. Why do ancestors become punitive? Fortes (1960) and others have suggested that what is transmuted into ancestorhood is not the "whole person" who dies, but the *authority* component, the power exercised by tribal elders. Ancestors are, as it were, projections of the authoritarian element in social life (cf. Kopytoff 1971).

It is also tempting to see, in the ancestral cults of lineage systems, a supernatural mirroring of the political order. A society without a centralized political system seldom has one or a set of deities worshipped by all its diverse lineages (though there are exceptions, such as the Nuer and their neighbors the Dinka; Evans-Pritchard 1956; Lienhardt 1961). The proliferated ancestral cults mirror the fragmented and acephalous political order. In centralized states, gods of a people and rulers of a people go hand in hand, reinforcing one another's authority; perhaps deities are, as Durkheim suggested years ago (1912), the social order writ large.

An older generation of anthropologists had been more interested in *totemism*. Totemism, a belief in a spiritual association between a clan or lineage or moiety and a bird, animal, or natural phenomenon, was discovered by the pioneer ethnographers in North America and Australia. It was taken to be very old, a survival of an early stage in the evolution of social organization and religion—and was therefore accorded great importance.

Totemism was later shown by Goldenweiser (1910) and others to include a diverse set of phenomena with but a few features in common; it was not a single institution. Now we see totemism, thanks to the work of Radcliffe-Brown (1951) and Lévi-Strauss (1962), as a recurring way of conceptualizing relationships in the social world in terms of relationships in the natural world. Crow and Eaglehawk moieties are conceived totemically not because members of the Crow moiety are like crows in some way and members of the Eaglehawk moiety are like eaglehawks, but because the *relationship between* the two moieties is conceived as like the relationship between the two bird species.

The natural world here serves as a means for symbolically representing the social world. As anthropological studies of symbolism and cosmology have become increasingly sophisticated, we have come to see this as one of many ways of symbolically representing social groups and categories. Studies of pollution, to take another example, have shown vividly how the human body may itself be used to symbolize the body politic—so that bodily substances and processes, and bodily orifices may be used in rites and prohibitions to express relationships between social groups and categories (Douglas 1966, 1970).

In the preceding pages, we have not only glimpsed some of the various possibilities for forming descent corporations patrilineally, and weaving them into adaptive social systems; we have acquired a range of analytical perspectives and technical terms that will serve us well in understanding matrilineal systems and other forms of descent organization. We are equipped now to understand how matrilineal descent works, and how matrilineal descent groups are woven into adaptive social systems.

4
MATRILINEAL DESCENT AND DOUBLE DESCENT

MATRILINEAL DESCENT SYSTEMS

Early cultural evolutionists found matrilineal descent fascinating. Endless drivel was published about "Mother Right" and primitive matriarchies (some of which has been revived recently in some of the worst literature on women's liberation). There is not a shred of plausible evidence that matrilineal descent is ancient and basic, and in fact it almost certainly has developed in various areas well within the last 10,000 years.

When that nonsense had been dismissed, matrilineal descent got much less than its fair share of anthropological attention. There were, to be sure, Malinowski's Trobriand Islanders and Fortune's Dobuans (1932). But matrilineal systems were in many ways slighted for 50 years of the study of social organization. Audrey Richards (1950) is a noteworthy exception, and there were a number of good individual studies of matrilineal systems in the years 1910–1960. But it seems fair to say that matrilineality was slighted badly theoretically, though less so than cognatic systems. Male chauvinism, pervasive in academic anthropology for decades, as in other disciplines, has been at least partly responsible. Matrilineal systems have somehow always been analyzed *in terms of* patrilineal systems, never the reverse. If the presentation adopted here seems to perpetuate that practice, it is partly for analytic convenience. We will see, for example, that in matrilineal systems a great many of the structural permutations possible in patrilineal systems simply do not occur. They are more constrained, more specialized. What the constraints are can be more clearly grasped if matrilineal systems are seen in contrast to patrilineal ones. But that does produce an unfortunate, and sexist, distortion. To correct or counterbalance this distortion demands a heretical rethinking of the male-oriented premises that have dominated the study of social organization for a century. It is a rethinking we badly need, the first steps to which have been taken by feminist anthropologists in the last several years; but this kind of a review demands a measure of orthodoxy.

When matrilineal systems finally began to get their due in the 1950s, and especially with the publication of Schneider and Gough's *Matrilineal Kinship* (1961), they still were depicted in terms governed by male-oriented premises. These premises have a substantial measure of validity, but they are also quite misleading when stated categorically. The premises, as outlined by Schneider (1961) and others, are:

1. There is no such thing as a matriarchy. In no known society have women held the key political power.
2. In a matrilineal society, it is thus always the case that the major political power of a descent corporation is in the hands of men: they comprise or control the "board of directors" of the corporation.
3. Therefore, matrilineal systems cannot be in any simple sense the mirror images of patrilineal systems. If men control political power in each, there is an asymmetrical relationship between the two forms.
4. Because men control key political power in a matrilineal system, it is misleading to speak of descent as passing from mother to daughter; instead, one can better think of descent as passing from a woman's brother to her son (Fortes 1959).

We will look shortly at some of the cases where male dominance was greatly tempered, if men were indeed dominant at all. However, at least in most matrilineal societies there are asymmetries that create internal strain and generate conflict. These are set out clearly by Schneider (1961), drawing insights from Richards (1950).

In a patrilineal system both political direction and replacement of members are managed through men. A patrilineal corporation can lose control of its women when they marry out; they are not structurally crucial, because a corporation's men provide leadership and also provide children who will succeed them and perpetuate the corporation. But in a matrilineal system, the corporation—given a rule of exogamy—faces a structural problem. If it is the male members who go to live with their wives, then they are dispersed; and the "board of directors" is scattered away from "corporation headquarters." If instead it is the women who marry out, leaving the men on their lineage land, then the corporation must somehow retain control over—and "get back"—the children of these women, who are the corporation members of the next generation.

This in turn generates what Audrey Richards has called "The Matrilineal Puzzle" (1950). A woman's ties to her husband are always at odds with her ties to her brother; and if the corporation is to endure and be strong, her ties to her brother must prevail over those to her husband at the crucial times. It is her brother who must keep primary control over her, because that represents the corporation's control over her children. Her sons must be her brother's heirs. In such a situation of structural conflict, marriage is almost inevitably fragile; divorce rates are likely to be high.

In a matrilineal society, the pattern of postmarital residence is crucially important. One possible pattern is for a husband to come and live with his wife in her corporation's place (uxorilocal residence). If this pattern is repeated in each generation, the localized group will consist of a set of matrilineally related women, the husbands of those women that are still married, and unmarried children of lineage women, plus lineage men who are not at that stage married and who have come back to home base (most often, after divorce or between marriages).

In such societies, women often exercise strong power in lineage matters, as we will see. However, the corporation is hard-pressed to maintain its strength if all or most of its adult men have scattered. Most often, the potential problem is largely avoided because in such societies the population is clustered into sizeable communities; and in any single community, several different matrilineages or matrilineal clans are clustered together. Thus the articulation of communities and lineages is characteristically either of Type III, or Type IV (pp. 42 and 43, Figures 16 and 17). The rule of descent-group exogamy and the rule of residence require a man to marry "out"—but that may be only across the plaza or a few hundred yards away. The men are thus not scattered in the way a diagram might suggest, and are close enough at hand to take an active part in corporation affairs. The Hopi Indians will serve to illustrate:

CASE 11: THE HOPI INDIANS

The pueblo-dwelling Hopi Indians have a highly intricate social and ceremonial organization. The major descent groupings are exogamous matrilineal clans, each tracing relationship to a particular animal, plant, or natural phenomenon. These clans are landowning corporations. They are also central in the elaborate ceremonial cycles, in which each has a special part to play and a special set of ritual paraphernalia.

The clans are segmented into unnamed matrilineages, localized in sections of the pueblo. The "core" of these local groupings is a line of matrilineally related women. A Hopi man joins his wife's household—

and she can send him packing any time she pleases. A typical household consists of an older woman (and her husband if she still has one),
her daughters and their husbands and children, and her unmarried sons.
Note that the husbands are outsiders, and that the senior woman's
grown sons have married and moved elsewhere. Thus, while the lineage
retains effective control over its women and their children, the adult
men are scattered as outsiders in their wives' households.

The system hangs together partly because of a complicated series of
crosscutting memberships and ritual obligations in other kinds of
groups not based on descent. But it also works because men, by marrying girls of the same community where they and their fellow clan
members live (which they can do because a number of clans are represented in a pueblo), manage to remain near their "real home" and to
participate collectively in their clan's ceremonial activities and corporate affairs. Thus the male "board of directors" of a matrilineal corporation functions in important situations even though the men are scattered around the pueblo in their wives' households.

The control men exercise over lineage affairs can easily be exaggerated. And in the domestic realm, the power of Hopi women is striking. Hopi extended family households are local cores of minimal
matrilineages in which resident men are outsiders—solid domestic
corporations, largely controlled by its senior women in everyday affairs.

Where the rule that men are to marry "out" means much further "out"—
that is, where corporation territories are more scattered—adjustments that
keep at least the few lineage men most central to the corporation's "board
of directors" at home may be possible. They may remain unmarried, get
divorced, bring their wives "home" (in an alternative residence pattern),
or otherwise manage to stay at or near corporation "headquarters."

This residence pattern begins to suggest some of the constraints that limit
the form and also the occurrence of matrilineal descent systems. Matrilineal
descent groups characteristically are found in societies that:

1. are predominantly agricultural;
2. have sufficiently high agricultural productivity to permit the sedentary
   residence of substantial populations;
3. have a division of labor in which women perform many of the key agricultural tasks.

Even in such societies, patrilineal or cognatic descent groups, rather than
matrilineal ones, are quite common. Moreover, a number of the features
fairly commonly found with patrilineal descent—deep segmentary hierarchies, centralized political systems, ranked lineages—are rarely found in

matrilineal systems (here, as in all realms of social organization, there are exceptions—e.g., the ranked subclans of the Trobriands, Case 13, below).

Another variation on the possibilities of matrilineal descent—a society where, as in Hopi, women exercise more power than Schneider's (1961) model suggests—is illustrated by the Iroquois of the American northeast.

CASE 12: IROQUOIS SOCIAL ORGANIZATION

The Iroquois tribes of the American northeast are a striking example of a "kinship state." The famous League of the Iroquois, a political confederacy the writers of the U. S. Constitution drew on as a model, was conceptualized as an extension of the uxorilocal extended family and matrilineage.

The Iroquois confederacy consisted of five culturally related tribes, the Onondaga, Mohawk, Seneca, Oneida, and Cayuga. Our knowledge of their social organization is clouded by a lack of details about pre-European times, and by diversity between and within tribes that makes simple generalization difficult. But a relatively clear (if inevitably too simple) composite emerges from the scattered and large literature.

The pre-European Iroquois tribes lived, at least for most of the year, in 12 or 13 large villages of between 300 and 600 (Fenton 1951:41). Seasonally, the component families left the villages to hunt and fish in smaller groups. The core of Iroquois kin groupings was the household group, a series of matrilineally-related nuclear families that together occupied a longhouse (pairs of families shared a fireplace in the central aisle). The women of this extended family collectively held tools and garden plots and worked together in the cultivation of maize and other staple crops. The men hunted and fished. However, the household was controlled by its senior women; because of the uxorilocal residence pattern, the men were unrelated outsiders who belonged to different matriclans.

A cluster of these matrilineally-related households comprised a matrilineage, which in turn was localized in a section of a village. As we will see, all or most lineages had male leaders chosen by their senior women. Matrilineages were in turn grouped into exogamous matrilineal clans. However, the clans—ideally, eight in each tribe— were apparently not localized in a single village: each village had matrilineages from several clans, each clan included matrilineages localized in two or more villages. Matrilineages were strongly corporate; belonging to the same matriclan entailed ties and obligations of kinship, including mutual assistance in time of conflict.

Among the Western Iroquois, the matriclans were divided into tribal moieties. Each moiety was represented in each village, and in many ritual contexts—notably mourning ceremonies—the two moieties had important and complementary roles. The potential fission between matrilineages and between matriclans was checked in part by this ritual dependence on members of the opposite moiety. Moreover, the pattern of clan exogamy and uxorilocal residence meant that men of different lineages were united in a single household corporation. And it meant that a man or woman had strong kinship ties with his or her father's matrilineage as well; that lineage also played an important part in a person's life, ritually and socially. The component lineages of a community were thus bound together by webs of intermarriage, hence of kinship, ritual obligation, and common interest.

Iroquois society was also held together by a remarkable political system, one in which women played a prominent part commensurate with their power in the domestic realm and their central role in the subsistence economy. The Iroquois Confederacy that united the 5 tribes was governed by a council of 50 *sachems.* These male chiefs, who acted to maintain peace and conduct "foreign" relations, held positions or titles that belonged hereditarily to particular tribes (with the balance weighted in favor of the Onondaga); and within tribes, to particular matriclans or matrilineages. Succession to a sachem title, when an incumbent died, followed matrilineal lines. But the actual successor was nominated by the women of the lineage or clan. Among the Western Iroquois, the nomination of a sachem was confirmed by the moiety to which he belonged, then by the opposite moiety. In the event that the new sachem was too young to perform his duties, they were performed in his stead by a senior woman acting as regent. The sachem titles were not all equal in power and prestige. The Onondaga tribe had the three most important sachem titles, including that of wampum keeper. The lesser sachem titles also had specific duties assigned to them.

The organization was remarkably simple yet efficient. The component tribes each had separate councils, composed of the sachems of the particular tribe. The council dealt with the internal affairs of the tribe. As in the League council, discussion was open, with a premium on oratorical skill; and council decisions were unanimous.

It is worth assessing the status and power of women in Iroquois society (see Morgan 1851 and Randle 1951). Randle's summary is useful:

> The extended family structure of the Longhouse, symbolized in the League, accounts for the function of the matrons to hold the chiefs' names in their clans and their consequent right to appoint and depose chiefs. Death feasts and mourning were the responsibility of the women. Women kept the white wampum belts which signified the chiefly names. [They had] the ability . . . to influence decisions of the council both directly through their speaker and indirectly through the weight of public opinion . . . since unanimity was necessary for a decision to act, any proposal unpopular with the matrons could be hindered by their disapproval. Indirectly, too, it is stated that the women could hinder or actually prevent a war party which lacked their approval by not giving the

supplies of dried corn and the moccasins which the warriors required. Village head-women are mentioned in myth, and though they may not actually have ruled villages, this concept reflects the power that women were thought to possess. The importance of clan matrons in deciding the fate of captives . . . is well known (Randle 1951:171–172).

The base of female power lay largely in their central role in subsistence: "Economically, the maintenance of the household was a joint undertaking, but the women had the chief responsibility in the care of the fields and the raising of the staple foods. Men and women cooperated in the clearing of new fields, after that the womens' group took over" (Randle 1951:172).

Morgan had observed that "the Indian regarded woman as the inferior, the dependent, and the servant of man, and from nurture and habit, she actually considered herself to be so (Morgan 1851:315). An early feminist had taken a different point of view: ". . . by comparison with the restrictions . . . obtaining among *civilized* people, the Iroquois woman had a superior position and superior rights" (Converse 1908: 138). Randle's observations—in 1951—sound as though they had been made twenty years later: "Behind the feminist movement as well as behind most male chauvinism is the concept that the difference between the sexes is always to be interpreted as inferiority . . . Iroquois men and women had separate and different culture patterns, different values and different life goals" (Randle 1951:173–74).

Just how we should interpret the political power of Iroquois women, extending from their power in the longhouse corporations, has been a matter of some controversy. Richards (1957) argues that the power of women in the political arena has been exaggerated by Western observers, from Lafitau through Morgan and Hewitt. She sees the interpretation of the Iroquois system as "matriarchal" as misleading; and she sees in the historical records evidence of an increasing role of Iroquois women in the political realm due to two centuries of bitter warfare and a resulting dwindling of the male population. We cannot confidently assess the political role of Iroquois women prior to European contact. It was clearly not "matriarchal"; but it is equally clear that the male "board of directors" was strongly shaped and guided by senior women.

An alternative and important pattern of residence in a matrilineal descent system is to have corporation women go to live with their husbands; but somehow, to get the children (at least the boys) back to their lineage territory, so the adult men of the corporation are grouped together. This is technically called viri-avunculocal (husband's mother's brother) residence. The Trobriand Islanders of Melanesia provide a fascinating example.

CASE 13: THE TROBRIAND ISLANDERS

The Trobriand Islanders are a Melanesian people living near New Guinea, practicing shifting horticulture and fishing and living in villages scattered through rich garden lands of their large island.

The garden lands are divided into territories. Each territory contains sacred places from which, mythologically, its ancestress is supposed to have emerged. From her are descended, in the female line, the members of a *dala*. Since the precise genealogical links are not known but the groups are strongly corporate, *dala* are known in the Trobriand literature as "subclans." A Trobriand subclan is a matrilineal descent group consisting of:

1. men related through their mothers, their mothers' mothers, their mothers' mothers' mothers, and so on;
2. the sisters of the men, and other women similarly related in the female line; and
3. the children of these women (but not the children of the men).

The genealogical structure of such a group is similar to that diagrammed in Figure 3, page 19.

Given a subclan, associated with the territory it owns by these traditions of emergence, let us see who lives there. Such a subclan is centered in a village, in its territory. Since the subclans are exogamous, husbands and wives do not belong to the same subclan. Who, then, stays in the subclan's village? Is it the women, who provide the continuity of descent and whose children provide the next generation of corporation members? Or is it the men, who control the "board of directors," and one of whom is its leader? Either the women or the men must marry out.

In the Trobriands, it is the women of the subclan who go away to live with their husbands. How, then, do their sons end up in their own subclan villages and lands, instead of their fathers'? The answer is that during adolescence, a time when boys are freely drifting in and out of sexual liaisons and are relatively independent, a boy moves away from his parents' household and goes to the village of his own subclan. His sister remains attached to her father's household until she marries. Note that ideally, as a man's own sons leave him, his sisters' sons are moving in to join him. The village, in this simplest case, thus consists of:

1. adult men and young men of the subclan;
2. their wives, who belong to different subclans; and
3. the young children and unmarried daughters of men of the subclan.

A subclan is ranked as either "chiefly" or "commoner." Within these "ranks" the actual prestige and power of subclans varies considerably. But whatever its status, the Trobriand subclan is a strong and enduring landowning corporation, with strict rules of exogamy.

Each subclan is said to belong to one of four "clans." The importance of these "clans" is obscure, but it is clear that they are vaguely defined social categories of subclans traditionally associated by matrilineal descent and having symbolic connections with certain bird and animal species. They are not corporate groups, and a single clan may include some of the highest-ranking and lowest-ranking subclans. The rule of subclan exogamy is extended in theory to all members of the same clan, but some marriages to clan members from other subclans do in fact take place, and sex relations with them are regarded as naughty but not outrageous.

The system as it has been outlined is simple and stable: one subclan owning one territory with one village in it, where male members and their families live. That relationship, validated by the myths of origin, implies great stability and permanence. In fact the Trobriand dogma of procreation, that denies a role to the father, asserts that the children born of the subclan are a sort of reincarnation of its ancestors, thus underlining the continuity of the social order.

But as we saw in dealing with patrilineal descent groupings, the real social world of real people is always less neat and stable than that. Descent corporations do not stay the same size; proliferation, dwindling, and extinction of lineages require mechanisms for groups splitting off, collapsing, and taking over one another's lands. At any time, the interests, strategies, and alliances of individuals and groups, and the variations of demography, require that residence and affiliation be more flexible and variable than the dogma would have it.

In reality, if we could look at the Trobriand social scene over a period of a century or two (before the introduction of transistor radios), the identity and arrangement of subclans and their territories would almost certainly shift drastically over that time span. One mechanism whereby this occurs is the branching off of a segment of a proliferating (and usually, an important) subclan so that it attaches to the village and territory of another subclan.

By this mechanism, many local segments of subclans are living in different territories from those where their ancestors are supposed to have emerged. Moreover, many villages are composed of two or three or more subclan segments. Sometimes the attached "immigrant" subclan segments outrank and politically dominate the original "owners."

A second adjustment of the Trobriand descent system to ecological pressures and the shifting complexities of social life concerns residence. On close examination, it turns out that a surprisingly large percentage of Trobriand men are not living in the village where their own subclan segment is based. Many are living in their fathers', fathers' mothers', or other villages. This does not mean that subclans as corporations are all messed up—only that a man can be an active member of his corporation even if he happens to be living somewhere else (Powell 1960, 1969a, 1969b).

Finally, the whims of demography are subject to human rearrangement, since a great many children are adopted into households other than those of their birth. This does not affect their subclan membership, but it shifts them into different households (often those of subclans other than father's or mother's) during their childhood.

Thus, as with patrilineal descent among the Smiths and Joneses, matrilineal descent in the Trobriands shapes strong corporate groups that solve many of the organizational problems of tribal life in this setting. By allowing flexibility, choice, and readjustment of living arrangements, it also permits effective adaptation to the changing pressures of an environment and the shifting tides of social life.

Near the Trobriands, on the Melanesian island of Dobu, an even more fascinating compromise of residence was adopted: husband and wife alternated annually between residence in her matrilineage's village (where he was a feared and insecure alien) and residence in his matrilineage's village (where she was an outsider). Fortune's description of the tensions involved is an anthropological classic (Fortune 1932a).

In many societies with matrilineal descent groups, the wife goes to live with her husband; yet the husband lives in his father's place, not in his matrilineage's territory ("viri-patrilocal" residence). If one traces out the implications of such a scheme, it would seem that lineages could not be localized. Neither the men nor the women of the corporation live together. Such systems, common in Melanesia and parts of Africa, are (as we will see) conventionally viewed as representing a late stage in the disintegration of a matrilineal system into a patrilineal or cognatic system; the matrilineage is no longer a strong corporation, but a kind of remnant category or debating society. But some detailed studies have shown that lineages in such societies can be localized and powerful to surprising degree despite a residence rule that ostensibly prevents localization.

CASE 14: SUKU MATRILINEAGES

The Suku of the Congo comprise a kingdom of some 80,000 Bantu speakers. The women are farmers, cultivating cassava, peanuts, and other crops; the men devote primary attention to hunting, though with the introduction of firearms game animals have become scarce.

Suku live in villages, traditionally with between 15 and 75 inhabitants.

The small villages were grouped by the Belgians into large villages of several hundred, but the old village groupings comprise separate blocs within the modern village. Villages are usually separated by several miles of garden land and forest.

Suku are organized in corporate matrilineages. The Suku term for matrilineal descent group, *kikanda*, has a range of referents, from a widely dispersed matriclan to successively narrow lineages. The primary lineage is the *kikanda* in its narrowest sense: an autonomous lineage of about 30 persons. This matrilineal group acts corporately vis-à-vis hunting territories and other property—and in the political arena, vis-à-vis other lineages. The lineage comprises living and dead, and acts as a sacred community as well as political and economic unit.

Yet postmarital residence among the Suku is normatively virilocal. How can Suku lineages act corporately if their male members disperse at marriage? The residence rule would seem to preclude lineage localization; neither the men nor the women of a lineage would be clustered together in space.

Each village is regarded as the traditional center of a particular matrilineage, the focus of its sacredness and ritual observances. True, roughly half the men in a Suku village are not members of the matrilineage supposed to be based there; but the other half, including the lineage headman and its most important men, do in fact live in the lineage center. How is this achieved?

First of all, the matrilineages are not exogamous (though a man is forbidden to marry a lineage member of his own generation). A substantial number of men marry young women who are fellow lineage members, so that their children reside in the lineage center (if the fathers are there, or come to live there). The lineage headman moves to his lineage center, before or when he succeeds to this office. The preference for marriage of a man to his father's sister's daughter results in a number of women moving to their *own* lineage center at marriage, and raising their children there (see Figure 22). Finally, when a man's father dies (or at least when his close paternal kin die), he may move with his family to his lineage center. It is at this stage of life, as a lineage elder, that his presence at "corporation headquarters" is most important for the political effectiveness of the lineage.

When a Suku woman marries a man in a distant village, she and her children may be too far away to maintain close relations with fellow matrilineage members and take part in lineage rites. This may in fact be the first stage in the establishment of a lineage segment in a new village. However, the segmentary relationship between the mother lineage and the offshoot lineage is preserved in ritual and genealogical tradition.

Among the Suku, then, a rule of descent and a rule of postmarital

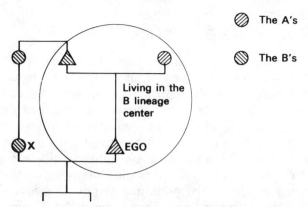

FIGURE 22   Father's Sister's Daughter Marriage among the Suku. A young man is living with his father in the father's lineage center (see text for an explanation of how the father would have returned in adulthood to his own B village). Ego marries his father's sister's daughter X. She comes to live with ego; but they live in the lineage center of her own B lineage. Thus ego's and X's children will grow up in their own lineage center. (Note that later, when ego is an elder and his father has died, ego and his wife might move to the A's village, where he could play an active part in lineage affairs.)

residence that would seem to militate against strong corporate descent groups are in fact worked out in a seemingly stable and viable pattern of residential alignment (Kopytoff 1964, 1965).

   Matrilineal descent systems, we have seen, span a broad range of diversity. Though many of these systems are well documented (see Turner 1957, Goodenough 1951, and Colson 1958 for further vivid examples), we still need further information about them and a deeper understanding (less dominated by male points of view) of how they work and how they have developed.

DOUBLE DESCENT SYSTEMS

Where two or more descent principles are used in the same society, usually only one of them is used to form corporate groups; the others define the distribution of other rights. But there are important, though comparatively rare, cases where both patrilineal and matrilineal descent are used to form corporate groups. You belong to your father's patrilineal group and your mother's matrilineal group. These are called *double descent systems*. But these are always *different kinds* of groups, important in different contexts. In one setting, it is relevant for you to act as a member of your father's group; in another setting, it is relevant for you to act as a member of your mother's group. The Yakö of Nigeria will serve to illustrate:

CASE 15: THE YAKÖ OF NIGERIA

The Yakö of Nigeria, living in large towns of as many as 11,000 people, are organized in a way very similar, at first glance, to our patrilineal Smiths and Joneses. A small patrilineage group, like the Elm Street Smiths, resides together in a compound. But whereas Smith streets were scattered in among Jones and Brown streets, Yakö compounds are grouped together into a cluster, a large local patrilineage that corporately owns land. Finally, a series of patrilineage clusters are grouped together into a clan, occupying a single "district" of the town. This correspondence between territories and segmentary levels recalls the Tiv (Case 4). The clans are exogamous, so a Yakö man's wives (he often has several) come from other districts.

Yet at the same time, the Yakö trace matrilineal descent; and any Yakö belongs to his mother's matrilineal clan. Whereas the patrilineages are concerned with real estate and ritual involving lands and first fruits, the corporate matrilineal clans are concerned with movable property, with legal responsibility for their members and rights to payments for their death, and with ritual involving fertility spirits. Any man belongs, of course, to his father's patrilineage and to his mother's matriclan.

Thus two different modes of corporate group organization, through patrilineal and matrilineal descent, fulfill complementary functions in different spheres of Yakö life. Since only full siblings normally belong to both the same patrilineage and the same matrilineal clan, people opposed in one situation may well be allies in another—hence helping to bind together the large Yakö communities (Forde 1950).

Although double descent systems are not common, we have good documentation of several others, such as the Herero of South Africa and the Yapese of the Pacific. It is noteworthy that in all these societies, postmarital residence is virilocal. Hence the patrilineages are localized, the matrilineages or matriclans are dispersed.

There is a potential confusion between double descent systems, where matrilineal descent corporations operate in addition to patrilineal ones (although sometimes they are not strongly corporate and act only in limited contexts), and systems where "complementary filiation" (or cognatic descent) creates a superficial convergence to them. The convergence comes because with "complementary filiation" a man has an interest in his maternal kin and their group. Goody (1961) tried to sort out the two in an important summary paper. But the fuzzy concept of "complementary filiation" led him to further confusions. The difference between a cross-cutting principle of matrilineal descent and a secondary principle of cognatic descent (Fortes' and Goody's "complementary filiation") shows up clearly in two places. Where

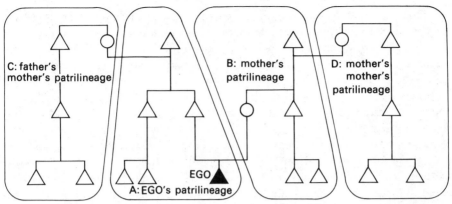

C: father's
mother's patrilineage

B: mother's
patrilineage

D: mother's
mother's
patrilineage

EGO

A: EGO's patrilineage

FIGURE 23 *Complementary Filiation.* Ego traces relationship to patrilineages B, C, and D as well as his own (usually in that order of importance).
Keesing (1970) has suggested that ego's relationship to these lineages through
female links may in many cases reflect a secondary principle of cognatic
descent, through which ego derives secondary interests.

cognatic descent is operating, a man has rights and interests through his
father's mother; in double descent systems he does not. And where cognatic
descent is operating, a man's strongest rights through his mother's side are to
her *father's* people and *patrilineage*; in double descent systems, his rights
through the mother are to her *mother's* people and *matrilineage*. The contrast is diagrammed in Figures 23 and 24.

The older anthropological literature on descent systems characteristically
noted at this stage some more complicated or peculiar forms, that were not
quite unilineal or not just unilineal.

First, there were the highly complicated "section" systems of Australian
Aborigines. One major line of interpretation was to see them as "bilineal" or

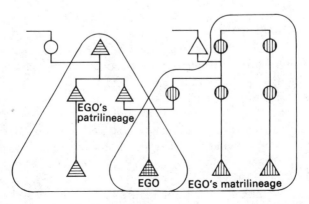

EGO's
patrilineage

EGO

EGO's matrilineage

FIGURE 24 *Double Descent.* Ego is not related to his father's matrilineage
or his mother's patrilineage.

"duolineal." That is, a principle of patrilineal descent and a cross-cutting principle of matrilineal descent operated simultaneously. Unlike a double descent system, where a man belongs to his father's patrilineal group and his mother's matrilineal group, an Australian section system was viewed as the intersection of both principles at once: a man belonged to one of four (or eight) sections that represented either two (or four) patrilineal descent categories cut in half by matrilineal moieties (Lawrence 1937; Murdock 1949). But as we will soon see, this interpretation has largely been superseded by more powerful theories of how Australian systems work. The older interpretation suffered from the disadvantage that the supposedly cross-cutting patrilineal and especially matrilineal descent categories—however clear they seemed on the anthropologist's diagrams—were often not culturally recognized by the Australians themselves.

Then there were several incompletely documented reports of descent systems that were based on "parallel" or "cross" descent links. The Mundugumor of New Guinea were reported by Mead (1935) to have a system of forming social groups called "alternating descent": men are supposed to belong to their mother's group, women to their father's, in what the Mundugumor call "the rope." How this works is unclear, and it seems unlikely that solid corporate groups are formed in this way.

The Apinayé of central Brazil were reported by their ethnographer, Curt Nimuendajú (1939), to be organized in four exogamous descent categories or *kiyé*. These *kiyé* functioned as "marriage classes": a man in a particular *kiyé* was supposed to marry a woman from only one of the other three *kiyé*. Moreover, the rule of descent was anomalous: a man belonged to his father's *kiyé*, and a woman belonged to her mother's *kiyé*—what has been called "parallel descent" in the literature. Various kinship theorists—Kroeber, Lowie, Murdock, and Lévi-Strauss among them—have commented through the years on this mode of descent and marriage alliance and its implications for theory. Yet Maybury-Lewis (1960), examining the systemic entailments of the rules Nimuendajú described, concluded that the *kiyé* could not in fact have functioned in the way reported. Recent field work by Roberto Da Matta among the Apinayé has confirmed Maybury-Lewis' skepticism (Da Matta 1973). There turn out not to have been any *kiyé*—Nimuendajú had confused two modes of grouping and coalesced them. These groupings turn out to have no corporate importance in secular affairs and have nothing to do with marriage rules: they are ceremonial categories operative only in certain festivals. Moreover, membership is based not on "descent" from father and mother, or on what Scheffler and Lounsbury (1971) call "parallel succession"; but rather, on relations through *foster* parents who are not close kin at all (Da Matta 1973).

Da Matta's reflections about Nimuendajú's errors can usefully apply to a number of other "anomalous" cases in the anthropological literature, such as the Banaro of New Guinea (Thurnwald 1916):

> . . . Little by little, social anthropologists are discovering that their fundamental task is not merely to describe the formal aspects of the social systems they study, but rather to analyze the application of formal rules in specific contexts . . . (1973:289).

On close examination, "anomalous" descent groupings and other elaborations of formal social structure have usually turned out to be not exotic ways of forming corporate groups, but models and symbolic systems in terms of which a people conceptualize their social world—models that correspond only indirectly if at all to the way groups are organized.

Finally, theorists dealing with descent systems had to come to terms with scattered reports of tribal peoples who—like early Teutonic peoples—were organized not on the basis of unilineal descent, but on the basis of bilateral kinship. Or so it seemed, from early reports on the Kalinga of the Philippines, the Maori of New Zealand, and others. The usual solution was to toss these societies into a leftover bag and forget about them.

The bag turns out on inspection to contains a substantial share of the world's societies; and these societies are highly diverse. That was the cost of classifying them on the basis of what they were not, rather than what they were. As we will see as we sort out these societies in Chapter 6, many of these systems turn out to be quite similar to unilineal descent systems. By confusing bilateral kinship with cognatic descent, theorists had overlooked the way cognatic descent can be used to form discrete corporate descent groups. Understanding how these cognatic descent systems work, and sorting out the other contents of the discard-bag, was a major challenge to social anthropology in the latter 1950s and early 1960s.

Another challenge of the same period—one that ties even more directly to our understanding of unilineal descent systems—was the study of *alliance systems*, including those of Australian Aborigines. We will glimpse the fascinating complexity of alliance systems and the heated controversy they have raised in Chapter 5; and then will return in Chapter 6 to examine cognatic descent systems and bilateral kinship systems.

5
ALLIANCE SYSTEMS

A rule of band exogamy in a hunting and gathering society means, in effect, that men of a group are renouncing sexual rights over their own women and acquiring rights over women of other groups. As Tylor (1889), Fortune (1932b), White (1959), and others had pointed out, a rule of exogamy makes bands interdependent on one another, hence it represents a major step in the direction of political integration. It was probably an old human innovation dating far back into the Paleolithic.

But as Lévi-Strauss (1949) pointed out, bands that renounced their women to acquire potential rights in the women of other bands would have been making a big statistical gamble. He sees as a likely early development the formation of alliance relationships between bands, such that they ex-changed women. Lévi-Strauss pored over ethnographies from remoter corners of the tribal world, from tribal pockets in India and Southeast Asia, from North Asia, and ancient China, to piece together evidence that such systems of marital exchange were ancient and basic.

Lévi-Strauss' massive book, belatedly translated as *The Elementary Structures of Kinship* (1969), has been harshly judged by recent critics (Scheffler 1970; Leach 1970; Korn 1973). But all students of kinship recognize its seminal influence on the field and the new insights to which it led. From his work (prefigured by the writings of several Dutch Indonesianists) has emerged the study of *alliance systems*—of systems of affinal exchange or prescriptive marriage.

We will examine the major modes of alliance. In the course of this quick survey, the points of controversy that have spawned a vast (and often nasty) literature will be noted. I will suggest that beneath this debate, which has seemed trivial and petty to nonspecialists, lie some important issues about the interpretation of human social life.

SYMMETRICAL ALLIANCE

The simplest, and probably oldest, mode of alliance involves the direct exchange of women between the men of two local groups. More widely, such systems can involve the exchange of women between two *kinds* of local groups, or the division of communities into two "kinds" of people (each of whom must acquire a mate of the other "kind").

Such direct or symmetrical alliance thus often takes the form of an *exogamous moiety* system. Men of moiety 1 marry women of moiety 2; men of moiety 2 marry women of moiety 1. Such a system can work whether moiety membership is determined patrilineally or matrilineally.

But specialists have learned that symmetrical exchange can work without exogamous moieties. The mode of kinship classification technically known as *Dravidian*, which we will examine in some detail in Chapter 7, divides a person's relatives into two classes ("our kind," or kin, and "the other kind," or affines). If each person's social world is conceptually divided in this way, symmetrical alliance (i.e., reciprocal marriages between the two "kinds" of people) can operate without exogamous moieties—in fact, without descent groups of any kind.

Such a division of two "kinds" or "sides" conceptually (with or without moieties) is technically called a *two-section system*. Two-section systems are found in such widely scattered areas as South India and Ceylon, North America, South America, and the South Pacific.

More complex forms of alliance systems occur among Australian Aborigines. We cannot here cover the great complexity of Australian kinship systems; and in any case, despite almost a century of anthropological debate, even the most basic principles of how they work are still very much at issue. Rightly or wrongly, Lévi-Strauss (1949) interprets these Australian systems as complex schemes for the exchange of women between local groups. We will illustrate one of the simplest Australian systems, the Kariera *four-section system*.

CASE 16: THE KARIERA OF AUSTRALIA

The Kariera were a hunting and gathering people, numbering about 750, living in a territory along the coast of northwestern Australia. The tribe, distinguished by minor differences in language and culture from its neighbors, comprised some 20 to 25 local groups. These local groups, of about 30 people each, are called "hordes" in the literature (Radcliffe-Brown 1913). They consisted of patrilineally related men, their wives (who, by the rule of exogamy, came from other groups), and their children. Each horde was tied to its territory through ritual association with its ancestors.

Each Kariera man or woman belonged to one of four named classes, known in the literature as "sections": he or she was Karimera or Burung or Palyeri or Banaka. These four sections fit into the scheme of hordes in pairs. Roughly half of the Kariera hordes (and here it is easiest to think only of their male members) consisted of Karimera and Burung men. Roughly half consisted of Palyeri and Banaka men. These two "types" of hordes were arranged in roughly checkerboard fashion (see Figure 25). Note that in the diagram the neat boundaries are artificially drawn; we do not know the actual boundaries of the KB (Karimera-Burung) and BP (Banaka-Palyeri) groups.

A man who is Karimera belongs to the same horde as his father. But

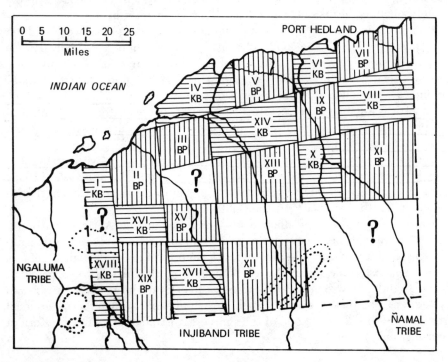

FIGURE 25   Distribution of Kariera Local Groups, from Radcliffe-Brown 1913. Idealized boundaries and shading added. (From Romney and Epling 1958. Reproduced by permission of the American Anthropological Association from the American Anthropologist. Vol. 60, 1.)

his father (and the other male members of father's horde in father's generation) are Burung. Though father is Burung, grandfather and other men of his generation are Karimera. That is, this distinction between Karimera and Burung sections alternates between generations. The other kind of horde containing Banaka and Palyeri sections similarly alternates generations (Table 3).

TABLE 3

Kariera Hordes and Sections

	TYPE 1 HORDE	TYPE 2 HORDE
	Karimera	Palyeri
GENERATION	Burung	Banaka
	Karimera	Palyeri
LEVELS	Burung	Banaka
	Karimera	Palyeri

Note that the sections, unlike kinship terms, are absolute, not relative. If we look from the standpoint of a Karimera man, Palyeri men are in the same generation (or one two removed) but other kind of horde; if we look from the standpoint of a Banaka man, Palyeri men are in the same kind of horde but a different generation (one up or one down).

There are no terms designating the units Karimera + Burung or Palyeri + Banaka (though they are so easy to distinguish analytically as patrilineal moieties that many anthropologists have misleadingly done so). Nor are there terms for the two types of hordes, except that a man may distinguish between "my people," (his horde and those with the same sections) and "they people," (those with the other two sections) (Radcliffe-Brown 1913, 1951:39; Scheffler, n.d.).

A man must marry a girl from the opposite "kind" of horde, but his own generation. Thus:

Karimera ♂ marries a Palyeri ♀, children are Burung
Burung ♂ marries a Banaka ♀, children are Karimera
Palyeri ♂ marries a Karimera ♀, children are Banaka
Banaka ♂ marries a Burung ♀, children are Palyeri

The system of kinship classification reflects this division of the social universe (though just how has been hotly debated by specialists). The kinship terms are basically Dravidian in type (see Chapter 7): that is, all relatives are divided into two categories, "cross" and "parallel."

They are further distinguished by sex and generation. The kin term *nyuba* denotes "cross" relatives of opposite sex and own generation. These include a man's mother's brother's daughter, father's sister's daughter, mother's mother's brother's daughter's daughter, and a great many other cousins—second, third, fourth, fifth, and others more distant. For a Karimera man, any Palyeri girl (unless she is in the grandparent or grandchild generation) is his *nyuba*; and these are the only girls he can legitimately marry. These include his first cousins, and among the Kariera a young man has a legitimate first claim on the daughter of his maternal uncle. Sister-exchange between two men of the appropriate sections is also a favored marriage arrangement.

The Kariera system can be analyzed to show a beautifully consistent and all-embracing fit between the section system, marriage rule, and kinship terminology (see, e.g., Romney and Epling 1958). This requires that a few troublesome details be swept under the carpet, and that a few convenient missing pieces be supplied (Scheffler, n.d.). It also ignores some comparative evidence. There are Australian tribes that have Kariera-like kinship terms but have no section system (or a quite different section system). There are tribes that have similar kinship classification but forbid marriage with first cousins, hence ruling out sister-exchange as a continuing pattern.

It seems best to view the section systems as a way some Australians invented, perhaps not very far in the tribal past, for conceptualizing complex kinship systems in simpler fashion. The alliance systems very probably are much older, and were conceptualized (as in South India and Melanesia) in terms of kinship categories (though the elaboration of section systems and the further complicating of alliance systems may have gone hand in hand). Kinship terms and section labels work in quite different, though complementary, ways. A given person is not simply a *nyuba* to all people in all settings: he is one person's *nyuba* (cross-cousin), someone else's brother, someone else's uncle, and someone else's grandson. But to all of them, he is a Karimera. But what a Karimera is (in terms of behaviors, rights, etc.) depends on what you are: if you are a Burung, a Karimera is one of "my people" (in a junior or senior generation); if you are a Palyeri, a Karimera is one of "they people," but a person whose sister you might marry (or whose granddaughter you might marry). The section terms simplify the system because to act appropriately to a person from another horde, perhaps a stranger, you do not have to know genealogical relatedness; you need only know what section he or she belongs to. For Australian tribesmen, who often spent part of their lives travelling on "walkabout" far from home, such a scheme was a great invention (Radcliffe-Brown 1913, 1930; Romney and Epling 1958; Scheffler, n.d.; Goodenough 1970).

The much more complicated "eight-section" system of the Aranda and some other Australian tribes works by, in effect, subdividing each of the sections into two. This produces four "types" of hordes (with a corresponding elaboration of the kinship terms). The marriage rule still requires that a man marry a cross-cousin. But the conceptual cutting in half of each of the four sections, to form eight, subdivides the Kariera-type cross-cousin category. A man must marry into a different "type" of horde from the one his father married into; hence the marriageable girls include second (and more distant) cross-cousins, but not first cousins. Aranda-type systems are by far the most common in Australia. Specialists have argued for years about why the sections are subdivided into eight. An interesting new development is the suggestion that over much of Australia, marital alliance involved not the exchange of wives between local descent groups, but the exchange of mothers-in-law. A young girl who is a young man's mother's mother's brother's daughter, or is classed with her in the kinship terminology, is bestowed on him *as his mother-in-law*. From that time onward, there is an avoidance relationship between them; but the daughters she later bears when she marries become his wives. Shapiro (1970) suggests that this practice has led to the subdivision of the sections so that ego and his mother-in-law will not be members of the same patrilineal group. He suggests that the even more complicated Arnhem Land eight section systems, some of which have asymmetrical marriage systems that have become battle-grounds for anthropological controversy (notably the "Murngin," who have been renamed "Wulamba" and now "Miwuyt" through no fault of their own) may similarly express patterns of mother-in-law bestowal (Shapiro 1970; see Goodale 1962, 1971).

As section systems spread (and that spread has been going on in historic times), sections have been adapted to or superimposed on alliance systems and kinship terminologies they did not fit very neatly. Thus, one cannot tackle an Australian kinship system with any assurance that there is a neat solution. Not only have tribes borrowed systems to keep up with the Joneses in the neighboring tribe, sometimes creating strange composites (one aborigine was released after some years in an Australian prison, only to find that his tribe now had a new marriage system and eight sections instead of four); but Aborigines were adept at circumventing their marriage system when they found themselves checkmated, and hence unmated, by the rules of their own game.

Barnes' recent comments on the "Murngin" are a useful caution to the aspiring Australianist:

> Aborigines, like anthropologists, enjoy making systems . . . and it is easier in Arnhem Land, as elsewhere, to make a model in the mind than to persuade one's neighbours to abide by its rules through the generations. If, as Lévi-Strauss maintains, totems are good to think with [see p. 60], then equally

subsections and kinship categories are good to play with. It seems likely that some Aborigines in northeastern Arnhem Land are still in a muddle about subsections and terminology, while others have a clear picture of how the system ought to work, as they see it (Barnes 1967:45–46).

ASYMMETRICAL ALLIANCE

Despite these complexities, Lévi-Strauss argues that the Australian systems still represent a *direct exchange* between local groups, such that the groups who are "wife-takers" are also "wife-givers." However, in Southeast Asia and a few other places there are tribal pockets where another mode of exchange is represented, which Lévi-Strauss calls *indirect exchange*. These systems became, in the late 1950s and early 1960s, a focus of great controversy in anthropology, particularly centering around the interpretations of Rodney Needham (1962).

The crucial rule in such systems is that a group that gives wives to yours cannot also take wives from yours. The system of affinal alliance is *asymmetrical*. For any given group, the social world is divided into wife-givers and wife-takers (along with some groups that share common descent with yours, hence are forbidden to intermarry with yours, by the rules of exogamy). Some of the confusions about such systems came because diagrams of such chains of asymmetrical alliance seem to imply "marriage in a circle," whereas things are in reality much more complicated than that. Some of them came because the rule of marriage was often expressed in terms of kin terms: you must marry your "mother's brother's daughter" (where in fact the kinship category also includes girls of any wife-giving lineage); and you cannot marry your "father's sister's daughter" (a category that similarly includes a wide range of girls in wife-taking lineages). Much debate has centered over what these *prescriptive* rules mean, and how sharply they differ from the common expression of preference for marrying a girl who stands in a particular kinship relationship. Further debate has arisen over "wrong marriages" in such a system (see Lounsbury 1962 and Maybury-Lewis 1965).

The picture that has emerged is of systems far more complex and dynamic than "marrying in a circle" would suggest. These societies are usually composed of many small localized patrilineages. It is these lineages that serve as "alliance groups" in the marriage system. The lineages may be ranked, and markedly unequal in status, as with the Kachin of Burma (Leach 1954), or they may be unranked, as among the Purum of Assam (Needham 1962). In either case, marriage becomes an instrument of political negotiation and status. A few marriages in each generation may serve to maintain the political status of lineages. Other marriages are less important and in some societies need not necessarily conform to the marriage rule.

From the standpoint of any single lineage, some girls may be non-marriageable because their lineages share common descent at a higher segmentary level. Some lineages may simply be too far away for marriages to be likely. But there remain two other crucial categories of lineages. There are those whose girls have married men of one's own lineage (they are "wife-givers") and those to which one's own has given women (they are "wife-takers"). <u>The basic marriage rule is that no other lineage can be *both* wife-giver and wife-taker.</u> While actual patterns of marriage may deviate from the ideal model, most "wrong marriages" (at least those that are politically consequential) are treated *as if* they were right ones, and hence simply readjust the shifting network of alliances. Such an alliance system is usually prominently reflected in the cosmological scheme of a people. The contrast between wife-givers and wife-takers is mirrored in cosmological dualisms (right–left, sun–moon) and in ritual symbolism. The Purum of Assam provide a useful (and much debated) example.

CASE 17: THE PURUM ALLIANCE SYSTEM

The Purum are a small Tibeto-Burman-speaking tribe living on the eastern border of India, numbering only about 300 when they were studied anthropologically. They live in four politically autonomous villages, each governed by its own council. The Purum are divided into five named, exogamous patriclans. Each clan is marked by special personal names, and each has a separate section of a village burial ground. The clans are in turn segmented into named patrilineages (two clans have four lineages, two have two lineages; the fifth is not segmented). Since some lineages are represented in two or more villages, a further division is relevant: a localized village lineage segment, the most important corporate group in marital alliances. Table 4 (below) shows distribution of lineages in the three villages for which we have data.

Purum marriage rules are phrased in terms of prescriptive alliance. Marriages are negotiated by the men of alliance groups—village patrilineage segments (e.g., the men of lineage 1, Julhung, of the Kheyang clan who live in Khulen village A). A marriage is a contract between alliance groups. From the standpoint of any alliance group all Purum lineage segments fall into three categories:

1. Fellow clansmen (unmarriageable by the rule of exogamy);
2. Wife-givers (lineage segments from which one's own group has received wives);
3. Wife-takers (lineage segments to which one's own group has given wives)

There may also be lineage segments that fall into none of these three, because no past marriages have been contracted with them. By nego-

TABLE 4

Purum Descent Groups (From Rodney Needham, *Structure and Sentiment.* Copyright © 1962 by the University of Chicago. Reprinted with permission of The University of Chicago Press.)

	CLANS	LINEAGES	VILLAGES		
			A	B	C
	Kheyang (K)	1. Julhung	+	+	+
		2. etc.	...	+	+
	Makan (MK)	1.	+	+	+
		2.	+	...	...
	Marrim (M)	1.	+	...	...
		2.	+	...	...
	Parpa (P)	———	+	+	+
	Thas (T)	1.	...	+	...
		2.	+	...	...
		3.	...	(extinct)	...
		4.	+	...	...

tiating a marriage with them, they can be converted into either wife-givers or wife-takers. The alliance rule is simply that no local lineage segment may stand in both wife-giving and wife-taking relationship to one's own.

The alliance relationships of Purum lineages are shown in Table 5. That is, the men of Julhung lineage of Kheyang clan (K_1) cannot contract alliances with other Kheyang lineages according to the rule of

TABLE 5

Scheme of Purum Alliances (From Rodney Needham, *Structure and Sentiment.* Copyright © 1962 by the University of Chicago. Reprinted with permission of The University of Chicago Press.)

$$Mk_2, M_2, M_4, P, T_1, T_2, T_3, T_4 \rightarrow \quad K_1 \rightarrow Mk_1, M_1, M_3$$
$$Mk_1, Mk_2, M_2, P, T_1, T_4 \rightarrow \quad K_2 \rightarrow M_1, M_3, M_4$$
$$K_1, M_2, P \rightarrow Mk_1 \rightarrow K_2, M_1, M_3, M_4, T_1, T_2, T_3, T_4$$
$$K_1, M_1, M_2, M_3, M_4, P \rightarrow Mk_2 \rightarrow K_2, T_1, T_2, T_3, T_4$$
$$K_1, K_2, Mk_1 \rightarrow \quad M_1 \rightarrow Mk_2, P$$
$$T_1, T_2, T_3 \rightarrow \quad M_2 \rightarrow K_1, K_2, Mk_1, Mk_2, P$$
$$K_1, K_2, Mk_1, T_1, T_2, T_3, T_4 \rightarrow \quad M_3 \rightarrow Mk_2, P$$
$$K_2, Mk_1, T_1, T_2, T_3 \rightarrow \quad M_4 \rightarrow K_1, Mk_2, P$$
$$M_1, M_2, M_3, M_4 \rightarrow \quad P \rightarrow K_1, K_1, K_2, Mk_1, Mk_2, T_1, T_2$$
$$Mk_1, Mk_2, P \rightarrow \quad T_1 \rightarrow K_1, K_2, M_2, M_3, M_4$$
$$Mk_1, Mk_2, P \rightarrow \quad T_2 \rightarrow K_1, M_2, M_3, M_4$$
$$Mk_1, Mk_2 \rightarrow \quad T_3 \rightarrow K_1, M_2, M_3, M_4$$
$$Mk_1, Mk_2 \rightarrow \quad T_4 \rightarrow K_1, K_2, M_3$$

exogamy. They receive wives from all the lineages to the left, give wives to all lineages to the right. Note that even this scheme, much more complicated than "marriage in a circle," is a simplification. For there are Julhung lineage segments in village A, village B, and village C. Although the same alliance rule pertains to each segment, the autonomy of the villages suggests that the politics of actually contracting and maintaining a pattern of alliances are managed separately by each Julhung segment. Unfortunately, our information on the crucially important questions of local politics and strategy is very thin.

This rule that wife-givers cannot be wife-takers is reflected in the kinship terms. All men of wife-giving lineages, regardless of generation, are classed together. All men and women of wife-taking lineages are classed together. (Such lumping of kin in different generations by a single kinship term is discussed in Chapter 7.) Girls and women of wife-giving lineages, in ego's generation, are classed as *nau* (so, too, are younger brother and sister, and younger cousins of ego's own lineage). This bears importantly on controversies about "mother's brother's daughter marriage." Mother's brother's daughter is a *nau*; and ego is supposed to marry a *nau* (and forbidden to marry a *tu*, one of whom is father's sister's daughter). But ego can marry *nau* who are in a different lineage or clan from the mother's, and who may not be genealogically related to the mother at all. To say that this is a system of "mother's brother's daughter marriage" or "matrilateral cross-cousin marriage" is sorely misleading. Note also that to look at the marriage rule from ego's point of view (who he or she can marry) is misleading: it is the parental generation of lineage men who do the negotiating. Moreover, even to say that "a man must marry his *nau*" would not suffice to define permitted marriages; for many of his *nau* are clan sisters, hence forbidden to him.

If we look at the sparse data on actual marriages, the inadequacies of describing the system in terms of "mother's brother's daughter marriage" are underlined. Of 54 marriages for which we have data, 26 (almost half) are with *clans* other than the mother's. Of the 28 marriages with a woman of the maternal clan, many are undoubtedly with women of different *lineages* (hence, alliance groups) than the mother's. And even where marriage is with a girl of mother's own lineage, from mother's own village, it may be with ego's second or third cousin, not mother's brother's daughter (see Scheffler and Lounsbury 1971:225). Although the majority of recorded marriages (43 of 54) take place within villages (so that marital alliance is most often negotiated between neighbors), some marriages—perhaps politically strategic ones —link otherwise autonomous villages together.

What happens when a "wrong marriage" is contracted? In the only apparent instance where the same group is both wife-giver and wife-taker to the same lineage, this seems to reflect the incipient segmentation of the lineage into two separate alliance groups. Where a man marries a girl in the wrong kinship category, what apparently happens (as in other such societies) is that the girl is ritually "adopted" into the "correct" category. The structural relations between affines make such a reassignment quite reasonable. Once a girl is married, she is formally separated from her lineage of birth; in important rituals she and her husband act as affines vis-à-vis her natal lineage (e.g., she makes beer ritually, and the women of her clan—to whose ancestors it will be offered—cannot help her). When she is buried, it is in her husband's clan's cemetery. If she was not in the proper category before the marriage, she enters it in her new status and new life.

This ritual relationship is but one element in a symbolic structure that reflects and reinforces the alliance system. Women are, in this scheme, the supreme good; and wife-givers are symbolically superior to their wife-takers. (Note that this status advantage is purely relative: the same men are wife-givers to one set of lineages and wife-takers to another.) Counterbalancing the cycling of women in one direction (from -giving to -taking lineages) is a flow of symbolically male goods, notably rice beer and pigs. A further return is the three years of bride-service after the marriage, where the groom lives with his father-in-law and provides work services. Moreover, a lineage's wife-takers provide a series of crucial ritual services (recall the out-marrying wife's role in sacrifices) to their wife-givers. Needham (1962) distills from a symbolic analysis a set of polarities expressed in many realms of Purum culture (see Table 6).

The alliance system of the Purum—and just how it works and can best be characterized—has been much debated in the literature. However, to understand the Purum social order we also would need to explore in detail political strategies at a local level, of which marriage alliances are one expression; and the elaborate symbolic system that weaves marriage into the structure of the cosmos (Needham 1962:82, 96; cf. Scheffler and Lounsbury 1971:209, 224).

The asymmetrical alliance systems of Southeast Asia were a focus of bitter anthropological debate in the 1960s. Whether the sharp line Needham draws between "prescriptive" and "preferential" fits the complexity of actual societies has been much debated; Lounsbury (1962) and then Lévi-Strauss himself (1966) have raised grave doubts. Particularly troublesome are cases where only a few politically strategic marriages in every generation need to follow the "marriage rule," in order to keep lineages in their proper alliance relationships; yet where (despite the preponderance of "wrong" marriages) the system is conceptualized in terms of asymmetrical alliance. Another problem that generated heated debate in the 1950s and 1960s was whether an opposite rule of asymmetrical alliance ("father's sister's daughter

TABLE 6

Symbolic Dualisms among the Purum (From Rodney Needham, *Structure and Sentiment*. Copyright © 1962 by the University of Chicago. Reprinted with permission of The University of Chicago Press.)

Left	Right
Front	Back
Affines	Kin
Wife-takers	Wife-givers
Female	Male
Below	Above
Feminine goods	Masculine goods
women	pigs, buffaloes
cloth	rice beer
loom	ritual services
domestic articles	labor (brideservice)
Mortals	Gods
etc., etc.	

marriage" or "patrilateral alliance") actually occurs in real societies (as well as on anthropologists' diagrams); and if not, why not. Here Lévi-Strauss (1949), Homans and Schneider (1955), Needham (1962a) and subsequent protagonists have tilted endlessly at theoretical windmills and one another (Korn 1973).

What is crucial in terms of kin group organization is that the lineages in an asymmetric alliance system are locked together in relationships of *perpetual affinity*. The exchange relationship between corporations endures across generations, and it need only be reaffirmed every several generations by another marriage. The system is in this respect quite different from the Smiths and Joneses, and most unilineal descent systems. Recall that only some members of the Elm Street Smiths became affines of the Olive Street Browns because of a marriage between them; and that the relationship became one of cognatic kinship in the following generation. In contrast, in an asymmetric alliance system all members of a wife-giving lineage are in an important sense affines of all members of a wife-taking lineage, and vice versa; and this relationship of perpetual affinity continues across generations.

In what came to be called "alliance theory," an attempt was made in the 1960s to rethink the relationships between corporations of African lineage systems such as the Tiv and Tallensi by looking at the marital contracts between corporations as affinal alliances akin to those in asymmetric alliance systems (Schneider 1965). Where particular corporations contract marriages with one another across generations, some insight is gained by this perspective. But by and large it is an empirical question how members of two lineages conceptualize their relationship to one another, how and for whom these relationships are changed by a marriage contracted between the lineages, and what becomes of these changed relationships in the following generation (see Figures 18 and 19 and accompanying text, p. 44). In these respects, <u>most African and other descent systems are radically different from the alliance systems of Southeast Asia.</u> The value of the alliance theory approach to unilineal descent systems in Africa has been that it led anthropologists to look more carefully at the interconnectedness of lineages as a *system*—to focus on the links between lineages (other than those segmentarily related by common descent) through time and space, rather than looking at lineages one at a time and seeing relationships between them from the standpoint of an individual and his network of kinship ties.

At this stage, we can return to those societies organized on bilateral and cognatic lines that for decades had been thrown into a leftover bag. The treatment they received for years, as a residue of anomalies and assorted leftovers, by no means accords with their theoretical importance or their frequency, as we will see. This treatment expresses a bias for formal organization, for corporate groups, for unilineal descent, that is built into the conceptual systems social anthropologists use. As we turn to the contents of the leftover bag, we need to be prepared to give them their due. We will return in Chapter 8 to a growing anthropological concern with (and sophistication about) informal social relations, counterbalancing the long preoccupation with formal blueprints and corporate groupings.

6

COGNATIC DESCENT AND BILATERAL KINSHIP AS ORGANIZING PRINCIPLES

As we have noted, tribal societies without unilineal descent systems were long relegated to a kind of negative leftovers bag of "bilateral" or "cognatic" societies. Radcliffe-Brown's rather contemptuous dismissal of such systems as a kind of "Teutonic aberration" was a major contributing factor. The technical vocabulary at hand, worked out by early kinship specialists (notably Rivers), predisposed anthropologists to focus on unilineal groupings, and left them ill-equipped to deal with societies without them. And that meant that the few detailed descriptions of "bilateral" societies were hard to interpret.

When a careful sorting out of the contents of the leftover bag was finally undertaken, it turned out that at least one third of all known tribal societies should have been in it. But in sorting them out, anthropologists discovered that it was a very mixed bag (see Murdock 1960).

COGNATIC DESCENT SYSTEMS

The societies that generated the most controversy in the sorting out process were those that seemed to have descent-based corporations very much like lineages, but where local dogma insisted that a person belonged (or could belong) to *both* his father's and mother's groups. Or, looked at the other way around, *all* descendants of the founder of a group, through any combination of male and/or female links, "belonged" to it.

That, of course, is *cognatic descent*. But as we saw earlier, if you draw out the implications you find that everyone "belongs to" many groups—those of all eight great-grandfathers, and more. How, then, can these be "groups" at all? Surely this is very different from unilineal descent systems, where groups are discrete and unambiguous, and where an individual clearly belongs only to one! In the late 1950s and early 1960s much controversy centered about how such systems work and how they should be classified (Davenport 1959; Firth 1957, 1963; Goodenough 1955; Scheffler 1964, 1965; Sahlins 1965; Peranio 1961; Forde 1963).

In the intervening years, we have found out through studying such societies in the field that the problems they pose on paper need not be serious problems "on the ground." Discrete or relatively discrete corporate groups *are* formed; and choice, flexibility, and multiple memberships are never as broad as the ideology implies. Organizationally, the challenge is to narrow down from the groups in which a person *could be* a member, and has secondary rights, to one where he actually *is* a member and has primary rights. Various mechanisms have turned up. One of the most important is parental residence. A married couple may have a choice of residence with husband's group or with wife's group; and the children then have primary interests in whatever group they grew up in. As Scheffler (1965) has pointed out, a person's potential "choice" to change groups is always constrained by political realities: the host group must choose to extend to him the privileges of membership (even though the ideology insists that he is entitled to them).

Especially in the Pacific, where such systems are most common, there is very often another force at work. In addition to a principle of cognatic descent, there is very often simultaneous recognition of a principle of patrilineal descent. This principle gives highest status or privileged position or strongest rights to those descent group members who are patrilineally descended from its founding ancestors, while the principle of cognatic descent insists that *all* descendants, patrilineal or not, are entitled to membership. Or there may simply be a cultural preference for affiliation with one's father's group. This results in patterns of affiliation that are predominantly patrilineal or at least patrilateral (cf. Figure 4, p. 23): other things being equal, a person will grow up with his father's people and affiliate with them; and through cumulative past affiliations most members will be agnates. To break this pattern is to weaken one's status and that of one's descendants. Yet strategies of gardening or feasting, or some quarrel, or parental death or fosterage, or feuding, or warfare, may lead a man to live with his wife's or his mother's people. As I have pointed out, when principles of cognatic descent and patrilineal descent are combined this way, the difference between the "patrilineal" Tallensi and the "cognatic" Kwaio of Melanesia is one of balance and emphasis (Keesing 1970):

CASE 18: THE KWAIO OF MELANESIA

The Kwaio of the Solomon Islands divide their mountainous terrain into dozens of small territories. Each is believed to have been founded by known ancestors some 9 to 12 generations ago. All cognatic descendants of the founding ancestor of a territory have rights to live there and use the land, and most of them raise pigs for sacrifice to the ancestors associated with that territory.

Yet a person obviously cannot live in, and have equally strong rights to, the many territories (often a dozen or more) to which he is related by cognatic descent. Usually he has strongest affiliation to only one territory and to a descent group based there. Those who are affiliated with the descent group form the nucleus of the landowning corporation; they are, so to speak, voting members with full rights. The other cognatic descendants, affiliated somewhere else, have secondary rights and lesser ritual interests.

How, then, does a person come to have a primary affiliation out of the large number of potential ones through his father and mother? In practice, he seldom affiliates with a descent group other than that of his father or mother. But which? First of all, a person who is patrilineally descended from the founding ancestor of a territory is considered to have the strongest rights in the corporation and the greatest say in its ritual affairs. Second, a woman normally resides in her husband's territory, and a person usually affiliates with the group with which he grew up as a child. All of these factors combine so that most people affiliate with their fathers' descent groups, and, cumulatively, most descent groups are made up mostly of patrilineal descendants of the founding ancestor. Cognatic descendants then have a secondary interest in the corporation. Yet in every generation, due to the circumstances of life history, some people grow up with their maternal relatives and affiliate with the mother's descent group. As long as they maintain an active participation in the corporation, they are treated as full members.

However, many men do not live in the territory where they have primary interests. In fact, Kwaio residence is quite fluid, and many men live in four or five territories or more in the course of their lives. They take an active, though secondary, interest in the ritual and secular affairs of several different descent groups. Depending on the context of the moment, a member of group A and a member of group B may both be participating in the ritual affairs or feast of group C, in which both have secondary interests based on cognatic descent.

Here the interplay of cognatic descent and patrilineal descent, the strategies of feasting and gardening, and the circumstances of life history produce solidly corporate yet flexible and adaptive descent groups (Keesing 1970).

Whether the "patri" bias in cognatic descent systems is patri*lineal* or merely patri*lateral* bears comment. The question has been debated mainly with reference to those New Guinea highlands systems (such as the Chimbu, Case 10, and the Enga) that look "patrilineal" but have a substantial number of men affiliated through female links (see page 57). If the preference for affiliation is patri*lateral* then a man who affiliates with his mother's group may in the short run be in a somewhat disadvantaged position. But if his son remains in that group (that is, the son affiliates patri*laterally*) and his grandson does the same, their position will be reinforced. This is the characteristic case for New Guinea, leading Barnes to suggest that "cumulative patrifiliation," not patrilineal descent, is operating (Barnes 1962; Scheffler 1974; Strathern 1972). But if the distinction is culturally made between *agnates* and *non-agnates* in the group (that is, in terms of patrilineal *descent*), then all the descendants of a man who has affiliated with his mother's group will be non-agnates. This is what happens among the Kwaio and the Choiseulese (Scheffler 1965; see Figure 42 and accompanying text). Non-agnates may eventually come to be classed as agnates in the course of the generations; but that reflects more general processes of editing genealogies to reflect present social relations.

Cognatic descent also occurs, along with a patrilineal descent principle, in a few societies where descent groups and/or social classes are ranked. The Polynesian Maori of New Zealand, with a much discussed cognatic descent system, will serve to illustrate:

CASE 19: MAORI SOCIAL ORGANIZATION

The Maori of New Zealand were grouped into a number of major tribes; the total population was about 100,000. Each tribe, an *iwi*, was led by a high chief who was descended directly by primogeniture from its founding ancestor. A tribe was named after the founder ("descendants of X"). The *iwi* was a territorial and political unit, whose component units united in war.

The tribes were segmented by traditional lines of descent into *hapu*. The *hapu* were cognatic descent groupings, characteristically spanning some eight to ten generations from the founding ancestor (Firth 1963: 30). *Hapu* were usually localized in villages (though large villages might contain segments of two or more *hapu*). Like the *iwi*, they were named after the founding ancestor (or sometimes, ancestress). They were not exogamous; in fact, there was a preference for marriage within the *hapu*. *Hapu* were in turn segmented into large extended families.

Residence was usually virilocal, but uxorilocal residence was fairly common, and divorced or widowed women often returned to live with their kin. When father and mother were from different *hapu*, children acquired rights of membership and land use in both (they also had secondary relationships to other *hapu* from whose ancestors they were cognatically descended). A person's residence and primary affiliation were usually in the father's *hapu*: partly because he was most likely to have grown up in his father's extended family household (and thus to have his firmest attachments there); and partly because in securing the highest possible status, patrilateral attachment conferred some advantage. Seniority of descent, and thus social rank, was reckoned according to closeness to the senior descent line, usually through oldest sons. However, female descent links could also be used to establish high status; and hence, affiliation through the mother (if she was of higher rank than the father) could confer social advantage. Childhood residence with maternal kin, or economic advantage, warfare, or personal circumstances could also lead to a primary commitment to (and domicile with) maternal kin. Thus the *hapu* could be viewed from two perspectives: as a corporate group with primary interests in an estate, consisting of men and women (and their children) domiciled there; and as a broadly inclusive cognatic descent category comprising the cognatic descendants of the founder of the *hapu*, including many domiciled elsewhere who kept their interests in the *hapu* alive, though latent. (Here recall the hypothetical example of the New England music festival, where those who acted as Patrons comprised a corporate group, with a wider category of those eligible by descent to be Patrons, many of whom lived elsewhere and did not take part.) The highest ranking member of a *hapu*—normally the oldest son of the oldest son in the senior descent line—was its chief and took the lead in ritual and in political decision-making. (Sometimes, if he were incompetent, another man might assume secular—but not ritual—leadership.)

It is not clear how important and carefully maintained was the ranking of different *hapu* within a tribe in terms of the seniority of descent. The structure of social classes—high-ranking chiefs, lesser men of rank, and commoners (in addition to landless slaves), with that status dependent on seniority relative to a line of descent—would seem to imply status differences between chiefs of different *hapu*, as well as between members of a *hapu*. Whether *hapu* themselves were ranked on any genealogical basis is not clear, and seems unlikely. Chiefly status conferred some economic and ritual benefits, but the social stratification did not entail great differences in power and privilege, and did not call for the marked deference characteristic of Hawaii, Tonga, Tahiti, and some other Polynesian areas.

Though we cannot reconstruct in detail how Maori society was organized, it is clear that the Maori combined a system of cognatic descent with the Polynesian pattern of ranking based on descent seniority (Firth 1957, 1963; Scheffler 1964; Biggs 1960).

There is no standard term for cognatic descent groups parallel to the term "lineage" for unilineal groups. Terms like "sept," "ramage," and "ambilineage" have been proposed; but none has gained general acceptance.

One characteristic difference between cognatic descent systems and unilineal descent systems is illustrated by the Maori case: in many cognatic systems, marriage is permitted within the descent group. In lieu of a rule of descent group exogamy, there is very often a rule specifying that a spouse must be at least a second (or third, or fourth, or fifth) cousin. (Recall, from parallel cousin marriage among the Bedouin [Chapter 3], that lineage exogamy is not universal in unilineal systems.)

As we will see, there has been much debate about whether the flexibility of affiliation implied in cognatic descent ideologies provides a mechanism for demographic adjustment and hence flexible ecological adaptation where land resources are scarce. For the moment, it serves to note that the kind of flexibility of residence achieved in Chimbu society (Case 10) under the mantle of patrilineal descent is given clear ideological recognition in cognatic descent systems. But cognatic descent systems in fact use only a small degree of the range of flexibility theoretically implied by the rules, therefore making possible discrete and solid corporate groups.

BILATERAL KINSHIP AS A DOMINANT ORGANIZING PRINCIPLE

When anthropologists got around to unpacking and sorting the discard bag of "bilateral" societies, they found that a substantial number of tribal peoples have worked out viable and adaptive social systems without *any* form of corporate descent group. Such forms of organization had of course been known for hunting and gathering peoples. A good many of them, like the Shoshoni (Case 1) and the Eskimo, use nuclear families as the primary social groups. The nomadic Könkamä Lapps, with their bilateral local groupings, illustrate another possibility (Pehrson 1954, 1957).

Among tribal agriculturalists, mainly in Southeast Asia, forms of social organization building on nuclear families and personal kindreds have developed that are fully workable and adaptive. Such systems are common in the Philippines, in parts of Borneo, and the Southeast Asian mainland.

It is worth emphasizing that in a great many unilineally organized societies, nuclear family groups are important and at least partly separate groups.
They may comprise separate or partly separate domestic or "hearth" groups
within an extended family or minimal lineage. (Where, as is especially
common in Africa, a man has several wives, each wife and her children are
likely to have a separate household.)

Personal kindreds also have some importance in a great many unilineally
organized societies. In settings involving life crises such as birth, initiation,
marriage, and death the group that gathers may include not only a person's
lineage mates, but also his or her bilateral kin. The action group is formed
from the kindred, not simply from the lineage.

These modes of organization can, in the absence of corporate descent
groupings, assume a much heavier "functional load." The family, as a
corporation, and the kindred, as a way of mobilizing larger groups when
needed, can provide adaptive solutions to the organizational problems of a
tribal society. A Philippine people, the Subanun of Mindanao, will serve to
illustrate.

CASE 20: THE SUBANUN

The Subanun are shifting horticulturists scattered through the mountains of Mindanao. They lack any formal political structure, and are
organized in no enduring communities larger than households and no
enduring kinship groups larger than the family. Yet they maintain
complex networks of kinship relations and legal rights that weave
families together. A family, consisting of parents and unmarried children, forms an independent corporation—owning property, sharing legal
accountability, and producing and consuming its own subsistence crops.

Two families arrange a marriage between their children, through
prolonged legal negotiations. Until an agreed bridewealth payment is
completed, the married couple must contribute labor to the bride's
parents, but in marrying they leave the parental families and found a
new and independent corporation. The family corporation formed by a
marriage, like a legal partnership, is dissolved by the death of either
partner (or by divorce), and its property is divided. Surviving members
or divorced partners—even a widow or widower with no unmarried
children—form a new corporation, however fragmentary: economically
self-reliant, and legally independent. Only remarriage or adoption can
incorporate survivors of a dissolved family into a new one. Once married, a Subanun can never return to his natal household. However, the
contractual obligation between parental families that sponsored the
marriage is strong and enduring: if one spouse dies, his or her household is legally obligated to supply another one if they can.

Marriage between close kin, even first cousins, is common. Given the independence of every family and the absence of larger corporate groupings, marriage of close kin entails few problems; every marriage is by its nature an "out-marriage." Each household lives in a separate clearing, as far from others as the arrangement of fields permits. Though 3 to 12 neighboring households comprise a dispersed "settlement," these alignments are only temporary. Any family is the center of a unique cluster of neighbors and kinsmen, bound first to the two families that sponsored its formation and later to the families with which it is contractually linked through marriage sponsorship. As Frake, their ethnographer, observes,

> Despite [the] network of formal and informal social ties among families, there have emerged no large, stable discrete socio-political units. . . . The Subanun family [is] . . . largely a "sovereign nation." But . . . the Subanun family is not a descent group. Its corporate unity endures only as long as does the marriage tie of its founders. The continuity of Subanun society must be sought in the continuous process of corporate group formation and dissolution rather than in the permanency of the groups themselves (Frake 1960:63).

Another Southeast Asian people, the Iban, provide an additional illustration of how social viability is achieved without corporate descent groups.

CASE 21: THE IBAN

The Iban or Sea-Dayak of western Borneo comprise some 200,000 rice-cultivating farmers whose social system—judging by their proliferation and spread in historic times—has been highly adaptive. Yet they, like many other Southeast Asians, do not use unilineal descent as a principle for organizing corporate groups.

The Iban live in sizeable communities, each one politically independent and occupying a defined territory. These communities include from as few as 30 to as many as 350 people. They are striking in that the inhabitants reside together in a single longhouse. The families in a longhouse are mainly cognatically related, but they do not comprise a corporate group. Their unity is expressed in ritual observances.

Each of the component families, *bilek* families, is strongly corporate. A *bilek* family is a separate economic unit, cultivating rice and other crops and owning heirloom property. And it is a separate ritual-unit, performing its own rites and having a separate set of magical charms and ritual prohibitions. Each *bilek* family lives in an apartment in the longhouse.

A *bilek* family typically contains three generations: a pair of grandparents, a son or daughter and the spouse, and grandchildren. The *bilek* family continues (unlike the Subanun family) as a corporation across generations. The device whereby this is accomplished is simple: at least one son or daughter in each generation stays put, brings in a spouse, and perpetuates the corporation. The other children characteristically marry into other households. Fission of a *bilek* family can occur when two of the children marry and bring their spouses in; one of the married children can claim his or her (equal) share in the family estate, and move the new nuclear family out to form a new corporation.

From the standpoint of a marrying couple, they face a choice of residence: either virilocal or uxorilocal. That choice determines which family corporation their children will belong to—hence, Freeman's term *utrolateral* ("either side") *filiation* (Freeman 1960:67). Sons and daughters in fact stay in the family home at marriage with approximately equal frequency. They must marry an outsider, since *bilek* families are exogamous. However, any first cousins or other more distant relatives who are in different *bilek* families are allowed to marry. Marriage is very much a matter of personal choice, and after the early years of marriage divorce is rare.

Larger action groups are predominantly recruited from within the longhouse, according to the context of the moment. As among the Subanun, this recruitment is usually along *kindred* lines. The personal kindred is an important social category for the Iban, including a bilaterally expanding range of kin. In theory, it includes all his or her known blood relatives; in practice, only fairly close kin are likely to be socially relevant. Kindreds, of course, overlap; they are not corporate groups. When life-cycle rites, feuds, or other intermittent events place a particular person on center stage, his or her kindred rally to provide the supporting cast (Freeman 1955, 1958, 1960).

That societies without corporate descent groupings are so common in the tribal world, and "work" so well, should not only warn us against treating them as residual "exceptions," it should throw into question the great emphasis on corporate groups and on formal or "structural" systems of social organization in social anthropology. Informal groups and networks, friendship as well as kinship, the texture as well as the structure of social life have increasingly commanded anthropological attention in recent years. We will return in Chapter 8 to these new and deeper probings into social relations.

First, it is worth looking at kinship terminologies: the ways relatives are classified. For decades anthropologists have assumed that the way peoples categorize their relatives represented some kind of mapping of the social universe. We will see that the ways of classifying kin in tribal societies are much less diverse than they might be, and fall into several characteristic patterns. But we will see that the search for general principles of correspondence between kinship terminologies and forms of descent, kinship, and marriage has led to frustrations as well as partial successes.

7
KIN GROUPS AND KINSHIP TERMINOLOGIES

KINSHIP TERMINOLOGIES IN TRIBAL SOCIETIES

Students of kinship have assumed for more than a century that the way a people classify relatives with kinship terms is related in some systematic way to their system of social organization. This assumption is based on several discoveries by Lewis Henry Morgan and his successors:

1. That kinship terminologies, though highly systematic, are highly variable; and that many peoples class relatives in very different ways than those familiar from European languages.
2. That these patterns fall into a quite limited number of major subtypes.
3. That the same formal patterns of classifying relatives occur in widely separated parts of the world (e.g., North America and Melanesia).
4. That these resemblances did not come primarily from historical connections, since closely related peoples often had very different terminologies and unrelated peoples often had similar principles of classifying relatives.

Through the years, different theorists have tried to account for these patterns of variation and distribution of kinship terminologies—for what societies have what type of kinship terminology—by stressing different elements of social organization: forms of marriage, modes of descent and kin groups, patterns of succession, the structure of the family, and so on.

Despite a century of effort, no anthropologist has succeeded in producing a satisfactory general theory of the systematic relationship between kinship classifications and social organization. As Radcliffe-Brown (1930, 1941, 1950, 1951) showed, one can "demonstrate" a beautiful fit between kin terms and kin groupings if one carefully selects the cases and does not look at the finer details. As Murdock (1949) showed, one can support an interpretation statistically if one looks only at the classification of closest relatives and worries only about statistically significant (not invariant) relationships. Needham (1962a, 1962b) and Leach (1958) have demonstrated a neat (but *ad hoc*) structural relationship between the particular features of one society and the details of its kinship terminology; but the striking parallels between terminologies on different continents are not accounted for in any systematic way in this insistence on uniqueness and *ad hoc* explanation. Recent efforts by Lounsbury and Scheffler to analyze these recurrent types on a global scale have clarified many details and even general principles previously overlooked. But their most recent work seems if anything to erode the expectation that kin terms systematically reflect forms of kin grouping or systems of marriage.

We can begin to see the challenge to explanation, and then why general theories have fallen far short of the mark, if we begin with a few first principles of kinship terminologies in the tribal world and then build up from there.

Most tribal societies have *classificatory* kinship terminologies. That does *not* mean that relatives of different kinds genealogically are lumped together under a single word—all kinship terminologies do that (e.g., English "cousins"). Classificatory kinship terminologies systematically class together *lineal* relatives (father, mother, grandparents) and *collateral* relatives (FB, MZ, FFB, etc.—where "FB" means "father's brother," and "MZ" means "mother's sister"; Z is used for sister to distinguish it from S for son). Collateral relatives are off to the side, the siblings or cousins of lineal relatives.

It is a very general (though far from universal) pattern in tribal societies that same-sex relatives are equated in the reckoning of kinship: this is how classificatory terminologies most often work. Consider these equivalences:

$$FB = F$$
$$MZ = M$$

That is, same-sex siblings of lineal kin are classed with them. Note what this means about classifying cousins:

$$FBS = FS = B$$
$$MZD = MD = Z$$

In other words, if FB is classed as equivalent to father, then his children are classed with father's children—as brothers and sisters. Similarly, mother's sister's children are classed as brothers and sisters.

Now note that this principle, successively applied, "collapses" more distant collateral relatives and makes them equivalent to lineals.

$$FFB = FF; \text{ therefore } FFBS = FFS = FB = F; \text{ and}$$
$$FFBSS = FFSS = FBS = FS = B$$

Note also that if you live in a society that classes relatives this way, you do not in fact have to perform all these operations in your head. Consider this little genealogy (Figure 26):

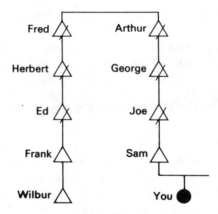

FIGURE 26   Kinship Reckoning.

Your problem is how you classify Wilbur, in a classificatory system. Do you have to know that Wilbur is your FFFFBSSSS? Not at all. All you need to know is that your father Sam and his father Frank classed one another as "brother." Knowing that, you know Wilbur is your "brother," and Frank is your "father." In turn, all Sam and Frank needed to know was that their fathers, Ed and Joe, were "brothers," and so on. In this kind of a system, where all kinds of distant relatives are classed with fathers and mothers and brothers and sitsers, genealogical knowledge is scarcely necessary. If you know how your father and mother are related to people, you know how you are related to them, and how you are related to their children. There is no mystery about that. *Why* tribal peoples use this logic of classification— what Wilbur and your "real" brother have in common—is another and harder problem. We will come back to it.

Let's back up for a minute. There are tribal and hunting and gathering societies that distinguish systematically between lineals and collaterals, as we do. They separate father from FB, who is an "uncle." But such societies are few (they include many Eskimo groups); and they tend to be societies where (as with us) there are no kinship-based corporate groups larger than the nuclear family.

But what about the societies with unilineal descent systems? What about peoples with cognatic descent, or peoples like the Southeast Asians who emphasize kindreds but have no descent groups? Most of them have classificatory terminologies. And these classificatory terminologies fall into three major patterns or types, each with variant forms. The differences between the three come in the way they classify the many relatives not affected by our first general principle—by the way they class MB, FZ, MFZ, MBD, and so on.

KINSHIP SYSTEMS: A COMPARATIVE FRAMEWORK

We can begin by distinguishing the three major "types." For the second and third, we will distinguish two subtypes. In the process, we can get some ideas about how and why they fit with particular forms of social organization—and also can glimpse why theories about this fit do not work very well.

TYPE I – Hawaiian

"Hawaiian" type terminologies deal with these other kinds of kin—MB, FZ, and so on—by being even more broadly classificatory. Instead of equating only same-sex siblings, Hawaiian terminologies "lump" relatives together by sex and generation. MB is equated with FB and F: in fact, all male relatives of the parental generation are classed with father; and all female relatives are classed with mother. All relatives of the grandparental generation are classed with grandparents. All relatives of "your" ("ego's") generation are classed with brother and sister. The result is a system with very few categories, each of which includes a very broad range of relatives (see Table 7).

Hawaiian terminologies characteristically occur in societies that do not have unilineal descent groups. These include both societies without corporate descent groups of any kind (societies that emphasize bilateral kinship and kindreds, as with the Subanun and Iban [Cases 20 and 21]); and societies that form corporate groups by cognatic descent (many Polynesians and Melanesians, such as the Kwaio). The general reason for the association of Hawaiian terminologies with bilateral kinship and/or cognatic descent systems seems fairly clear: in a unilineal descent system, paternal and maternal kin have very different relationships to ego (whether descent is patrilineal or matrilineal). If descent is matrilineal, for example, mother and MZ are members of your lineage; but FZ is not. In a bilateral system, on the other hand, ego is likely to have more or less similar relations to both paternal and maternal relatives.

TABLE 7

Categories in a Hawaiian System*

GENERATION +2	"Grandfather"	"Grandmother"
GENERATION +1	"Father"	"Mother"
GENERATION 0	"Brother"	"Sister"
GENERATION −1	"Son"	"Daughter"
GENERATION −2	"Grandson"	"Granddaughter"

* Some words of caution are in order. The English kin terms ("father," etc.) do not adequately translate the categories of the system—they are used to ease the burden of the reader in relating these categories to his own. For "father" we might better write "male relative of first ascending generation." Also, grandfather and grandmother are often lumped together in a single category. Sometimes there is a single word which designates grandparent *and* grandchild—that is, any relative two generations up or down from ego. Such terms are called "self reciprocal" (as with "cousin"—"cousin").

It is worth observing that few societies have Hawaiian terminologies in this "pure" or ideal form: most actual systems of classifications have some twist of their own or deviate in some respect from the ideal type. Most Western Polynesian and many Melanesian societies with cognatic descent groups have terminologies that are neatly Hawaiian except in one respect: there is a separate "uncle" term for MB (he is not classed with FB and F, though FZ is classed with MZ and M). In these societies (e.g., the Kwaio, Case 15), cognatic descent is combined with a strong tendency to affiliate with the father's group. Thus, for most people MB is a special kind of relative complementary to and different from the relatives on the father's side.

TYPE II – Dravidian-Iroquois

Let us review for a moment. The principle of same-sex equivalence lumps a series of collaterals together with lineals: FB and FFBS (and many others) with father; MZ, MMZD (and many others) with mother; FBC and MZC with siblings; a man's BC with his children, and a woman's ZC with her children. These collateral relatives who are structurally equivalent with lineals can be called *parallel* relatives.

There remains a class of relatives not equated with lineals by the same-sex sibling equivalence principle, which we can call *cross* relatives. (This distinction is overridden by the more general lumping of Hawaiian systems.) These include MB and FZ; MBC and FZC; and a man's ZC and a woman's BC.

The second major mode of kinship classification, Dravidian-Iroquois, distinguishes cross from parallel relatives in each of the middle three generations (+1, 0, −1 generations). Thus MB is distinguished as "uncle," and

FZ is distinguished as "aunt." Reciprocally, a woman distinguishes her BC as "nephew" and "niece"; and a man distinguishes his ZC as "nephew" and "niece." Ego distinguishes a class of "cousins" (his or her MBC and FZC) from the parallel relatives who are equated with siblings.

The terms "parallel" and "cross" have long been used to apply to cousins, as in Figure 27. Parallel cousins are the children of a pair of brothers or of a pair of sisters. Cross cousins are the children of a brother and sister.

It was noticed decades ago that these distinctions seemed consistent with unilineal descent (Lowie 1928). If descent was patrilineal, MB would be in a different lineage. F and FB would be in your own; FZ would be in your lineage and M and MZ would be in a different one. But note that this requires some mental flip-flops. For if descent is patrilineal, FBC and your siblings are in your lineage and MZC are in the other one—yet they are all classed together as parallel. The longer you play games with this mode of "explaining" why the cross-parallel distinction fits, the less well it works. One way out was to say that Dravidian-Iroquois terminologies reflect a pattern of "cross-cousin marriage" or "sister-exchange" where a man marries his MBD/FZD. Trace out the relationships and that seems to help: MBD and FZD turn out to be the same person; and if two brothers married two sisters in the first generation, FBC and MZC would turn out to be the same people (see Figure 28).

Unfortunately, many societies that distinguish cross and parallel kin and have unilineal descent groups show no sign of such a marriage system, past or present. And no marriage system ever really works this way, despite ideologies that sister exchange is appropriate: the number of brothers and sisters never works out right except on anthropologists' diagrams.

Another early line of explanation was that the classing of collateral kin with lineals by the same-sex equivalence principle (FB = F, MZ = M,

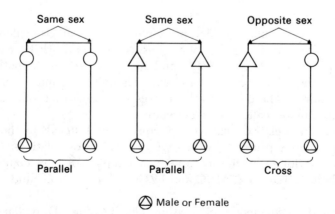

FIGURE 27   *Cross and Parallel Cousins.*

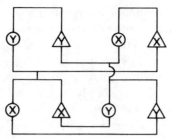

FIGURE 28   Sister Exchange.   Descent is patrilineal; the X's are one descent group, the Y's another.

FBS = B, etc.) reflected the levirate and sororate as forms of marriage. If a dead man's brother appropriately married his widow, and a dead woman's sister appropriately married her widower, then the equating of the two brothers and two sisters, from the point of view of their children, would seem to make sense. Unfortunately, the terminological mergings of same-sex siblings are found in many more societies than are the forms of marriage supposed to explain them. Moreover, as we saw (p. 43), these secondary marriages are simply a logical expression of marriage as an enduring contract between corporations.

Matters improved somewhat in recent years when anthropologists finally noticed that the Dravidian-Iroquois terminologies fall (as the hybrid label suggests) into two separate and quite different subtypes. The difference comes quickly into view if we look at how collateral relatives more distant than parents' siblings and first cousins are classed as either cross or parallel.

TYPE IIA – Dravidian   Notice that the principle we have given for distinguishing "cross" from "parallel" relatives works for the siblings of ego's parents and for first cousins—but it does not tell us whether ego's *parents'* first cousins are cross or parallel, or which of ego's second and third cousins are cross and which are parallel. The different subtypes of these Dravidian-Iroquois terminologies (two common subvarieties and one or more rare ones) differ in the way they distinguish between cross and parallel at these wider ranges.

The Dravidian subtype is commonly (but not always) associated with a requirement that a male ego marry a woman who falls in the "cross-cousin" category. It is often associated with exogamous moieties (whether matrilineal or patrilineal). And it is often marked by the terminological equivalence of in-laws (affines) with those consanguineal (blood) relatives who would be identical if cross-cousins consistently married one another. (Thus a man's wife is often classed with "female (cross) cousin," father-in-law is classed with MB, and mother-in-law is classed with FZ.)

This has led to a conventional interpretation of Dravidian terminologies as reflecting a symmetrical mode of alliance or prescriptive marriage (Chapter 5). This symmetrical alliance may be conceptualized in terms of exogamous moieties ("our side" vs. "their side," where the marriage rule may simply require marriage with a relative on the opposite side, in one's own generation). But the "sides" may simply be implicit divisions of each person's universe of relatives into "kin" (my kind of people) and "affines" (the other kind of people, with whom we marry). Such a terminological division has been called a *two-section system* (Chapter 5, p. 79). A Dravidian terminology has been seen as a terminological expression of such a system, as in Figure 29 (such interpretations have been most extensively developed by Dumont (1953, 1957, 1968) and Needham (1962b).

In Figure 29, the class of men shown in white marry the class of women shown in black; and the class of women in white marry the class of men in black. These classes may, but need not, be culturally recognized as moieties. Nor need a rule of descent be recognized at all. Here, however, ego classes his relatives in categories 2, 4, 6, 8, 10, and 12 as "kin" (my kind of people); and his relatives in categories 3, 5, 7, 9, 11, and 13 as "affines" (the other kind of people). Categories 1 and 14—grandparents and grandchildren—

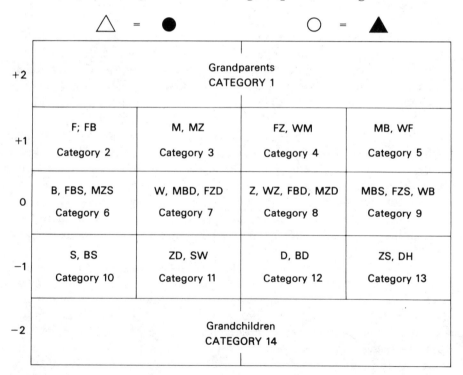

FIGURE 29 A Dravidian Kinship Terminology as a Two-Section System. (This is an idealized terminology where ego is a man. See text for explanation.)

are not differentiated as either kin or affines (the distinction is characteristically neutralized in such terminologies in ±2 generations). Note also that in this idealized Dravidian terminology, all of ego's in-laws (W, WF, WM, etc.) are equated with his consanguineal relatives (common but far from universal).

Note here that there is a disparity between the "kin" versus "affines" distinction and the "parallel" versus "cross" distinction. Ego's mother and mother's sister are *parallel*; but they are "affines," not "kin," according to the two-section system interpretation. FZ is *cross* but falls into the "kin" side. This need not be a contradiction, though it precipitated an early confrontation between Radcliffe-Brown and Dumont. The latter would deny the relevance of the parallel versus cross distinction as we have drawn it for the +1 generation (Dumont 1953).

But we have still not made clear how more distant cousins are defined as cross or parallel. We can illustrate this with a system with patrilineal moieties, in the classification of second cousins. Here ego is a male of the white moiety (Figure 30).

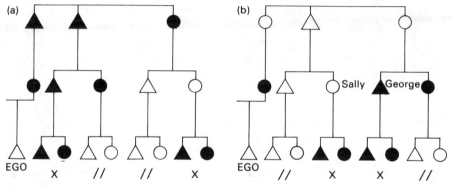

FIGURE 30   Cross and Parallel in a Dravidian Terminology. (These diagrams show ego's matrilateral second cousins. X = cross, // = parallel.)

Note that with every change of sex of a linking relative, cross versus parallel changes. Every intervening link is critical in affecting the classification of the relative on the end of the chain. Note, however, that ego need not know all of the genealogical connections in between (for third and fourth and fifth cousins, that would be even more complicated). Rather, all our ego would have to know (even if there were no culturally-recognized moieties) is whether his parents class their kin in their generation as cross or parallel. Ego has to know that his mother classes Sally (in 30b) as "cross" and classes George as "parallel." He knows then, by the rules of the game, he classes Sally with FZ and thus that her children, like FZC, are his cross cousins. He has to know that his mother classes George as parallel; hence that he classes George as MB, and thus classes George's children with MBC, as cross. The same principle allows ego's mother to class her third and fourth cousins as cross or parallel, and hence allows ego to classify their children (his fourth and fifth cousins) as cross or parallel, even though he has no idea what genealogical links connect him with them.

And this points to difficulties in the two-section system, or alliance, interpretation of Dravidian terminologies. For they not only occur without moieties, they occur in societies with or without lineages, even in societies with cognatic descent groups (Moala: Sahlins 1962) or with no descent groups (Ceylon:Yalman 1962, 1967). They occur with or without a rule for marriage with a cross-cousin, whether a first cousin or anyone in the "cross" category in one's own generation. (In Deuba, Fiji, a man is required to marry a woman to whom he is not related at all.) Thus the system of alliance is not necessarily associated with the kinship terminology it is supposed to explain. There are also many Dravidian terminologies where the equivalences between consanguineal (blood) relatives and in-laws the alliance model leads us to expect are absent (Scheffler 1971).

There are also problems in the meanings of the terms. Consider the terms we classed at the outset as "niece" and "nephew" (a man's ZC, and a woman's BC). Alliance theorists, looking at a male ego, have interpreted the terms as meaning (in a patrilineally structured system) "male (or female) in −1 generation, opposite section" (that is, for a male ego ZC are "affines"). But for a female ego, the terms would mean "male (female) in −1 generation, own section" (that is, for a female ego BC are "kin," not "affines"). Yet in most Dravidian terminologies, the same words are used by male and female speakers for "niece" and "nephew": the alliance theory requires us to conclude that the same words have different meanings depending on the speaker's sex. These and other difficulties in the "two-section system" interpretation are summarized by Scheffler (1971). He argues that present explanations of Dravidian terminologies are demonstrably inadequate; that there is no convincing alternative; and that we can probably expect no single explanation to cover all cases.

In Australian four-section systems, kinship terminologies are basically Dravidian with some special twists: within a line of descent, members of alternate generations are often lumped together by the same term. In an eight-section system, the cross-cousin category is divided in two, with only one of the two kinds marriageable (a subcategory that includes some second cousins, e.g., MMBDD, but no first cousins).

TYPE IIB − Iroquois   A quite different way of classifying cross and parallel, used in Eastern North America and widely in Melanesia, was belatedly noticed by Lounsbury (1964b).

In this mode, cross or parallel status is not determined by the intervening chain of genealogical links. Whether a relative is cross or parallel depends only on the last connecting link at each end of the chain. Thus any male relative on the father's side and in his generation is parallel, and so are his children. Any female relative on the mother's side and in her generation is parallel, and so are her children. Any female relative on father's side and in his generation is cross, and so are her children; any male relative on mother's side and her generation is cross, and so are her children. For first cousins, Dravidian and Iroquois terminologies thus class kin similarly.

But look at the case with some second cousins (in the Dravidian system shown in Figures 31a and b, descent is reckoned matrilineally; ego is female, cross relatives are hatched).

Although Iroquois terminologies are widespread, and generally associated with unilineal descent groups (either matrilineal or patrilineal), we as yet have no clear idea of how (or even *whether*) they reflect social groupings or marriage forms. They are *not* generally associated with or reflective of cross-cousin marriage. However, there are apparently some Iroquois terminologies where the equivalences are made between consanguineals and in-laws that are supposed to be a concomitant of Dravidian alliance systems. Since the wider structure of Iroquois terminologies is incompatible with the "two-section system" interpretation, this further erodes any easy explanation of Dravidian terminologies on the basis of alliance systems.

Type I (Hawaiian) and Type II (Dravidian-Iroquois) terminologies (and all other kinship terminologies) must deal with the classification of siblings. Classing them all together as "sibling" does not seem to partition the social world finely enough. But how, then, to make a finer sorting? Our way, using the criterion of alter's sex (that is, the sex of the relative being classified) to distinguish "brother" and "sister," is one solution (recall that in most tribal societies, the sibling categories are stretched to include some collateral relatives that we would class as "cousins"). But it is far from the only way.

Another commonly used criterion is relative age. Especially where inheritance, succession, or authority within the sibling group is defined in

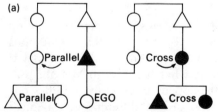

(a)

DRAVIDIAN: Here cross and parallel depend on the sexes of intervening links.

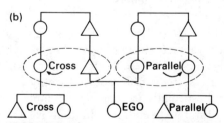

(b)

IROQUOIS: Here cross and parallel depend only on whether the sex of the circled pair is the same or opposite. Cross and parallel turn out just the opposite of the Dravidian classifications.

FIGURE 31 A AND B.   Cross and Parallel, Dravidian and Iroquois.

terms of birth order (either for brothers, or for both brothers and sisters), ego may use one term for older siblings, another for younger siblings.

Another criterion is relative sex. A very common principle for classifying siblings and parallel cousins in the tribal world, especially common in societies with unilineal descent groups, is for ego (whether male or female) to distinguish between "sibling-same-sex-as-me" and "sibling-of-opposite-sex." Thus, if *glob* is the word for the first category in a tribal language, a woman calls her sisters and female parallel cousins her *glob*; and a man uses the same word for his brothers and male parallel cousins.

These criteria can be combined in various ways. So, for example, a person's same-sex siblings may be distinguished by relative age while all opposite-sex siblings are classed together; or males may be distinguished according to relative age while female siblings are not.

In understanding these and other distinctions between kinship categories in the tribal world, it is always a useful question to ask what distinctions in legal status or role relationships they reflect. But the quest for perfect correlations and easy generalizations seems doomed to frustration. We will return to this question shortly.

TYPE III – Crow-Omaha

Dravidian-Iroquoïs systems—however puzzling and complicated—are structurally simpler than the last major subtype prevalent in the tribal world. But Crow-Omaha systems have been much analyzed and much debated, and the student who aspires to study kinship with any seriousness should keep plowing ahead.

Crow and Omaha terminologies, first of all, are exact mirror-images of one another (i.e., with all the sexes reversed, the classifications are identical). That is one thing that makes them so fascinating. So when we talk about one, it is like talking about the other upside down and backwards. That means that it is equally convenient to start with either. Crow systems will do for openers.

TYPE IIIA – Crow   First of all, in Crow systems the same-sex sibling equivalence principle we began with operates; so that those equations (FB = F, FBS = B, etc.) we are familiar with are still found. What makes these systems different and funny looking is what happens to MB and FZ, and especially to their descendants. What happens thoroughly muddles our cultural expectations, in that relatives who are in different genealogical generations are classed together. (We do that with uncles, aunts, and cousins; but we can distinguish those who are a generation out of alignment as "great aunts" or "cousins once removed.")

In a Crow system the basic principle of cross-generation equivalence or generation "skewing" is that a woman's brother and her son are treated as equivalent in reckoning kinship (Figure 32).

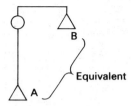

FIGURE 32   Crow Cross-generational Equivalence.

Note that A and B are *matrilineally* related to one another. As Lounsbury (1964a) has shown in the definitive comparative treatment of Crow-Omaha systems there are several subvarieties of Crow terminologies that treat this equivalence of A and B in slightly different ways. However, all of them entail a characteristic skewing of cousins. MBC are equated with BC (who for a man are equated with his own children) (see Figure 33).

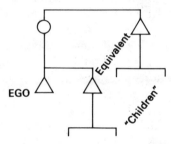

FIGURE 33   Crow Equations.

In some but not all Crow systems, MB and B are classed together as well; in others, they are equated only as connecting relatives, so that their children (but not they themselves) are classed with the same term (see Figure 34).

Let us look the other way around.

Sam classes both Fred and Arthur as "son" (by the above principle). Therefore, Fred classes Sam as "father," but so does Arthur. Note, then, what is happening: a man classes his MBC as children. These "children" then class their FZS as "father." Generations, as we reckon them, are a bit muddled. Let's see what happens when ego is female, by looking at Sally (Figure 34). Sally classes Fred as "brother's child" or "nephew." She classes Arthur the same way (due to our equivalence principle). Looked at the other way around, Fred classes Sally as "father's sister" or "aunt." So does Arthur: he has "aunts" in his own genealogical generation.

In most Crow systems the equivalence of a woman's brother with her son works more widely. Thus a person's mother's mother's brother's children are equated with brother's children as well. (Note the logic here: MMBC = MMSC [because MM's brother is treated as equivalent to her son]; and MMSC are the same as MBC; and MBC are, as just seen, equated with

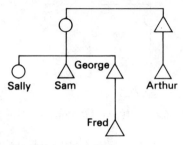

FIGURE 34   Crow Kinship Reckoning (1).

BC.) Figure 35 diagrams this relationship from Sam and Sally's standpoint. Sally and Sam class Herb as "brother's child," along with Fred and Arthur. Correspondingly Sam is Herb's "father" and Sally is Herb's "father's sister," even though they are a genealogical generation lower than Herb.

The result is that in a Crow system a line of *matrilineally related men* are equated in reckoning kinship: usually it is the *children* of these men who are actually classed by a single term (Figure 36). Here Sally is ego.

Years ago, kinship theorists noticed that Crow systems were found in societies with matrilineal descent groups; and they noticed that this seemed to make sense. It was suggested that the terms we labelled "father" and "aunt" should in fact be translated as "man of father's matrilineage" and "woman of father's matrilineage." Since that was a different corporation than ego's own, it made sense that in a strong lineage system their common corporate identity overrode the differences in generation: they were all lumped together. The terms we labelled "child" and "brother's child" should in fact be translated as "child of man of own matrilineage."

As Lounsbury (1964a) points out, there are some flaws in this interpretation. Moreover, some Crow terminologies are found in societies without any matrilineages. One could sustain the "unity of the lineage" interpretations only by assuming that the matrilineages had disappeared but the Crow terms had lingered on (or that the ethnographer was wrong).

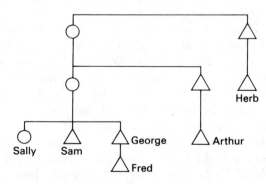

FIGURE 35   Crow Kinship Reckoning (2).

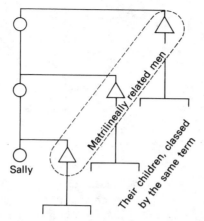

FIGURE 36   Crow Kin Classes and Matrilineages.

Lounsbury (1964a) has another interpretation. The nucleus of the Crow terminology is the relationship between A and B on Figure 32 (i.e., between a woman's brother and her son). They are equated in reckoning kinship, Lounsbury thinks, because A appropriately succeeds to B's status. The status involved often would be adult standing in the matrilineage. But it might also be some other political or legal right (e.g., rights over property, the right and obligation to marry B's widow, etc.).

TYPE IIIB – Omaha   Omaha terminologies are Crow terminologies with a sex-change operation. The nuclear principle is exactly opposite:

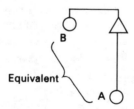

FIGURE 37   Omaha Cross-Generation Equivalence.

A man's sister is equated with his daughter in the reckoning of kinship. Note that A and B are *patrilineally* related to one another. In most Omaha terminologies, A and B are not themselves equated, but their children are. Thus, in Figure 38, Mary is in most Omaha systems classed by Robert as "father's sister" ("aunt"), and Brenda is classed as "sister" (in a few Omaha terminologies they would both be classed as "sister"). Mary's children and Brenda's children are all "sister's child" to Robert (Mary's children are classed by Brenda as "children").

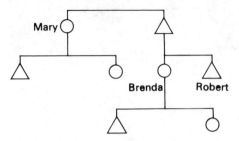

FIGURE 38   Omaha Kinship Reckoning (1).

And looking the other way around, Jeff and Wilma class Robert as "mother's brother," as do Brenda's children. And Jeff and Wilma class Brenda as "mother" (see Figure 39).

As in a Crow terminology, this extended across generations even further (Figure 40): Robert classes Linda as "sister's daughter," Brenda classes Linda as "daughter." Robert is Linda's "mother's brother," Brenda is Linda's "mother."

Note the logic of equivalences here in terms of the basic principle that a man's sister is equated with his daughter: FFZD (Linda)$\rightarrow$FFDD$\rightarrow$FZD (because FD $=$ Z)$\rightarrow$FDD$\rightarrow$ZD.

The result of such equivalences is that in an Omaha system a line of *patrilineally related women* are equated in kinship reckoning so that their children are classed by a single term (Figure 41).

As with Crow terminologies, the traditional explanation was the "unity of the lineage": the terms we labelled "mother" and "mother's brother" should be translated "woman of mother's patrilineage" and "man of mother's patrilineage." And the terms we labelled "child" and "sister's child" should be translated as "child of woman of own patrilineage." The unity of the lineage, seen from outside, transcended the generation differences between the members of mother's patrilineal descent group.

Unfortunately, as Tax (1937) and Lounsbury (1964a) have shown, there are Omaha kinship terminologies in societies without patrilineal descent groups. Again Lounsbury would interpret Omaha terminologies as reflecting

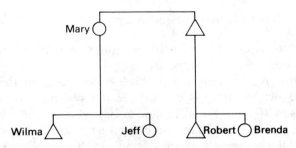

FIGURE 39   Omaha Kinship Reckoning (2).

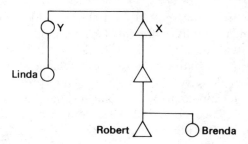

FIGURE 40   Omaha Kinship Reckoning (3).

a woman's succession to some elements of the status of her father's sister; that status might, but need not, be adult membership in the patrilineage.

An interesting and unresolved technical issue in the study of kinship concerns the kinship terminologies of societies with asymmetrical alliance systems, such as the Purum (Case 17) and the Kachin. Characteristically, these systems have terminologies where ego equates a line of patrilineally related women across generations; and equates a line of patrilineally related men (their brothers); and these categories extend to include members of other lineages that are in a "wife-giving" relationship to ego's own. Reciprocally, men and women of lineages in a "wife-taking" relationship are classed together across generations. The genealogical equivalences in such systems are essentially the same as those of an Omaha terminology, with this additional twist: that in-laws are terminologically equated with blood relatives that are structurally equivalent according to the rules of marital alliance (thus WF = MB, etc.).

The question is this: are these systems best considered as Omaha terminologies with the added special rule for equating in-laws with blood rela-

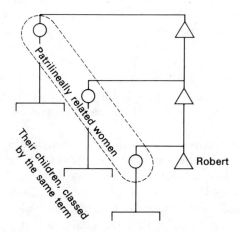

FIGURE 41   Omaha Kin Classes and Patrilineages.

tives (as Scheffler and Lounsbury [1971:190 ff] would have it)? Or are these terminologies fundamentally different (in lumping together broad categories of "wife-givers" and "wife-takers" to define the modalities of alliance) from Omaha systems, despite the surface resemblances (as Leach, Needham, and Lévi-Strauss would have it)? Lévi-Strauss' interpretation is unequivocal: "Although certain terminological resemblances may be noted, as far as their mode of functioning is concerned, those systems are as widely dissimilar as, say, fish and whale" (Lévi-Strauss 1965:18).

This divergence of interpretation prefigures the contrast between "genealogy" and "category" interpretations of kinship terminologies to which we will shortly turn.

Some variant of these three (or five) types of terminological systems—Hawaiian, Dravidian-Iroquois, or Crow-Omaha—is found in the majority of tribal societies. The first, as we noted, is preponderant where cognatic descent or bilateral kinship is used to form kin groups; the latter two types, each with two variants, usually occur in conjunction with unilineal descent groups. Anthropologists argue not only about the fit between a particular kinship terminology and a particular form of social organization, but about the general pattern of association between them. Given the general correlation between patrilineal descent and Omaha kinship reckoning, for example, why do some patrilineage systems have Omaha terminologies while others have Iroquois terminologies? Such questions are not yet satisfactorily resolved.

A common way of seeking to establish a fit between kinship terminologies and social systems has been to assume that kinship categories label social roles. Those relatives who appropriately act in a particular way vis-à-vis ego—whether that is an avoidance relationship (e.g. "mother-in-law") or an authoritarian one (e.g., "father") or one of closeness and support (e.g., "grandfather")—in a particular social system are classed together. Collateral kin who are terminologically equated with lineal kin have similar (but more distant or attenuated) role relationships. The importance of kin terms as role labels has been underlined by many recent studies which have shown how usage of kin terms often is adjusted to fit roles, rather than following "correct" genealogical classification. Since FFFBDS may well be the same age as ego, not the age of ego's grandfather with whom he is correctly classed genealogically, ego may (in some situations and in some societies) class him as "brother" instead.

But despite the obvious relationship between kinship classification and social roles, close inspection of most kinship systems reflects only a partial "fit" between role system and kin terms (see Keesing 1969). It may often be the case, as Scheffler (1974) and Lounsbury (1964a) suggest, that the classing of collaterals with lineals reflects not equivalence of the roles they play toward ego, but the fact that the collaterals are potential *successors* to the roles appropriately played by lineals. We will return to these issues in the next chapter (pp. 128–129).

This question is one side of a more general problem that has generated much recent controversy and dominated discussion of kinship theory. It takes us back to where we began: to the general classificatory principle of the equivalence of same-sex siblings (according to which FB = F, FFFBSS = F, etc.). When FFFBSS and F are classed by the same kin term, are we to translate that as "father" and say that the term has been *extended* to FB and FFBS and FFFBSS? (Presumably such extension would imply that they are in some sense socially equivalent, or that collateral kin constitute potential successors to elements of parental status.) Or are we instead to translate the term as "patrilateral relative of first ascending generation," and say that FFFBSS and F equally well fit this meaning? There would thus be no "extension" involved. The meaning is simply broadly categorical.

These two major ways of looking at these modes of classifying relatives in unilineal descent systems dominate the modern literature. These, popularly known as the "genealogy" and "category" positions, seem radically opposed.

Proponents of the *category* position, notably Leach and Needham, argue that in unilineal descent systems tribesmen conceptualize their social universe in very different ways than we perceive ours. Where we, with our emphasis on cognatic kinship, see webs and chains of genealogical connection between individual relatives, tribesmen see their world in terms of structural relations between social groups (or categories of people). Anthropologists have erred, they feel, by looking at kinship terminologies in unilineal descent systems as genealogical networks connecting individuals. Rather, a whole set of people who stand in a particular social relationship to ego (as potential spouses, wife-givers, members of a lineage, or residents in a village) will be classed together, regardless of their precise genealogical connection (Needham 1972; Hocart 1937).

Proponents of the *genealogy* position argue that reckoning of kinship in genealogical terms is universal, and apparently an old and basic human invention (Scheffler 1972; Scheffler and Lounsbury 1971). The kin groupings of unilineally-organized tribal societies act as a kind of overlay that adjusts or skews the mode of genealogical classification. Particular marriage rules, lines of succession or inheritance, or other forms of social equivalence or substitutability may lead particular types of relatives to be terminologically equated. The classification of primary relatives is extended to more distant relatives by rules of genealogical equivalence, and extended metaphorically to nonrelatives and deities. But the basic principles of kinship reckoning, in unilineally as well as bilaterally organized societies, are genealogical.

The controversy rages and resolution does not seem imminent. The prospects for establishing sweeping systematic relationships between kinship groups or marriage systems and modes of kinship classification appear to be dwindling. Closer scrutiny has forced us to see the nasty details that undermine previous theories. We are forced to *ad hoc* explanation of each case, to skepticism about systematic regularities, or to explanatory sleight of hand in defending general theories against painful evidence.

8
KINSHIP
AND
SOCIAL
RELATIONS

The ethnographers who studied tribal societies in the first half of this century, and before, preserved a valuable record of many ways of life now vanished beneath the juggernaut of "civilization" and "modernization." For hundreds of tribes, we have records of the formal blueprints of kinship structure—lists of clans, rules of marriage and residence, kinship terminologies. These were easy to elicit and easy to preserve on the printed page. But for all but a very few of these people, we know little about how kinship was used in everyday life. And in recent years, social anthropologists have realized that the subtle patterning of informal social relations, and the place of kinship in this patterning, pose central theoretical challenges.

Some of these challenges have risen to view in modern urban settings and complex and modernizing societies: the formal structure of "the system" has melted away, but kinship continues to affect patterns of social relations in crucial ways. But others have risen to view as anthropologists have belatedly recognized that life in tribal societies entails the same complexities of social relations—shifting of rules, roles, and strategies from situation to situation, informal networks of friends and allies—as life in our own society.

In this chapter, we will glimpse some recent explorations of kinship and social relations. We will see how new light has been shed on the place of kinship in social systems (patterns of relations between people) and in cultural systems (systems of ideas—of symbols, beliefs, rules, and plans).

121

KINSHIP IN SOCIAL RELATIONS:
NETWORKS, STRATEGIES, AND BEHAVIOR

For many years, social anthropologists have observed a gulf between the way peoples say kin should act toward one another—ideal standards or norms—and what they actually do. Close relatives, or fellow clansmen, should support one another, cooperate, avoid quarrels, and so on; yet the anthropologist often observes enmity, not amity, subversion not support, and feuding, not solidarity. What, then, to do conceptually about this apparent gulf between the ideal and the actual?

One solution has been to see behavior as primarily based on individual self-interest, as based on strategies for goal attainment. Kinship is, as it were, the idiom in which political interests are advanced and economic goals are maximized. When statements about the rules are made in natural settings (rather than as idealizations or rules of thumb told to an anthropologist), they themselves constitute political acts (Barth 1966; Leach 1961). The players of the serious games of social life follow strategies, form coalitions, and advance goals through and within—but also around the edges of—formal systems of kinship grouping. Barth (1966) argues strongly that in an important sense it is individuals pursuing their goals that create and sustain "the system." "The rules" and "the system" are in a sense epiphenomena; we turn things backwards if we start with them and try to explain the behavior of individuals as a product of (or deviation from) the system. The gap between ideal and actual recedes if we focus on actual behavior and the motives and strategies that generate behavior.

As we will see, studying informal networks of kin, friends, neighbors, and allies has become increasingly necessary in urban settings and situations of sociocultural change where the formal groupings have largely dissolved but ordered social life goes on. The development of methods and theories for systematically mapping and analyzing social networks has been a major advance in recent social anthropology (see Barnes 1971a; Whitten and Whitten 1972; J. C. Mitchell 1969; Bott 1971).

In their concern with social relationships, these approaches represent a continuation of British social anthropological tradition, though emphasis has shifted from jural rules and formal groups to behavior and informal networks. Another line of rethinking follows a more traditional American concern with *cultures*, as ideational systems.

KINSHIP IN SOCIAL RELATIONS:
CULTURAL RULES AND ROLES

In a classic 1951 monograph and subsequent papers, Ward Goodenough proposed that the cultural knowledge underlying social relations could profitably be analyzed in its own terms (Goodenough 1951, 1956). By cultural knowledge he meant shared conceptions of what "things" there were in a people's world, of what the rules and strategies—public and explicit, or unstated and implicit—were that governed and guided the games of social life. What are the "rules" (akin to the rules of a grammar) whereby a people make decisions about social relationships, about classifying individuals and groups, about rights over land and property?

Goodenough argued that the principles for making decisions, the alternative courses open to native "actors," might be quite different from those used by anthropologists in *a priori* schemes for cross-cultural comparison (1956). One had to map their culture in its own terms—in terms of the unique structure of a people's own conceptual world.

Cultural analysis of social relations has opened important new insights. For example, it has been shown that the same set of principles for making decisions may have widely different statistical outcomes under different ecological or demographic conditions. Imagine a people with a particular cultural system for categorizing the world, making decisions, forming groups, and relating to one another. In the course of their migrations, one group settles on an island that is large, mountainous, and ecologically rich but has no flat coastal land or lagoon. Another group settles on a small, flat atoll with a rich lagoon. Within a generation or two, the first group may live in scattered homesteads and reckon descent cognatically, with a highly flexible pattern of residence and kin group affiliation. Yet on the other island, people have grouped into two large villages and are organized in strictly patrilineal lineages. Yet the cultural principles remain the same; it is the circumstances in which decisions are made, the situations to which the "rules" are applied, that have produced distinctive patterns of social organization.

The example is not far-fetched. It has been demonstrated by Keesing (1967) and others that the same society may be "more patrilineal" or "more cognatic," depending on the demographic circumstances that happen to prevail. Harold Conklin and C. O. Frake, two linguistically-influenced anthropologists who explored the analytical paths first opened by Goodenough, have compared the cultural principles for making social decisions in two Philippine societies (see Case 20). One of these societies has descent groups, the other does not; yet the cultural "rules" regarding social groups and property were remarkably similar. Why, then, the descent groups in one and not in the other? Eventually they concluded that coconut palms grow in one place and not in the other: the descent groups (admittedly not very important ones) are the result of the same rules applied to a particular productive tree one group has and the other does not.

Such a cultural perspective, viewing the system in terms of its own unique structure and categories, has important limitations. Cultural "rules" constitute part of a social-cultural system that must be ecologically viable; cultures change in response to ecological pressures if their behavioral outcomes are maladaptive. Moreover, as the network and maximization models remind us, it is human individuals who make the "rules" and who follow, bend, or break them.

But cultural analyses of social relations are helping anthropologists to penetrate to a deeper level of understanding and to see that tribal societies are less different than our own than traditional modes of analyzing social structure would lead one to expect.

Anthropologists have given "lineages" and other kin groupings a false concreteness. They "exist" in the minds of the people in a society; and they often have a unified corporate identity in the same way that the General Motors Corporation or Westchester County has. But anthropologists have tended to imagine lineages as being solid groups out there in the world, each composed of real warm bodies; and to imagine these groups as "building blocks" out of which a "social structure" is built.

They are beginning to perceive that the real warm bodies move from one social situation to another, as we do; and that many of the things people do, places they go, and action groups they temporarily join have little or nothing to do with their membership in descent corporations.

Situational contexts are crucial. An example from the Kwaio (Case 18, above) vividly illustrates how the role a person is enacting in a particular situation determines the part he or she will play; and how this may not neatly correspond with membership in a descent group.

> One of my subjects is an agnate in descent group A and he is priest for the A's though he has not lived with them since infancy. He grew up and has always lived with his mother's kin, from descent group B. In the course of a mortuary feast our man was giving, a leader from group A approached from the left and presented him with a major valuable, which he accepted with his left hand. At the same moment, a man from B approached from the right and presented another valuable to him—which he accepted simultaneously with his right hand. Our subject was acting at the same moment as both an A and a B—and no one was confused. This is, of course, the limiting case where dual membership is expressed simultaneously. Yet in the course of a feast or marriage, an individual often acts as a member not only of more than one descent group, but of half a dozen other [descent categories]. Status in each case is clearly labeled, according to context (Keesing 1968b:83).

This case also illustrates how some of the seeming ambiguities of affiliation in cognatic descent systems, or among "patrilineal" peoples such as the Chimbu (Case 10), are resolved.

> Confusion and conflict of interest are avoided because ego's status is defined by context. One day ego behaves as a member of A, another day he may behave as a member of B, C, or D. Descent-group membership does not, at most times, demand some exclusive allegiance, such as residence. It merely includes ego in a social category from which groups are crystallized

in certain defined contexts. What is required to make such a system work is a situational sorting out, or clear labeling, of statuses, and a set of principles for making decisions in those situations where two allegiances conflict or where presence is required in two different places at once (Keesing 1968b:83).

Seeing the real warm bodies in a tribal society as moving from situation to situation, and enacting different roles and expressing different affiliations in different situations, can give an illuminating new perspective on the texture of social life. It enables us to transcend the false concreteness of many earlier approaches, and hence helps to close the gap between formal blueprints of the "social structure" and real people doing things together. In Kwaio society, for example, I have analyzed the action groups that crystallize in different settings—in feast-giving, in fighting, in ritual, and so on—as the enactment of different *roles*. A person acts as "feast-giver" one day, as "member of fighting party" the next. In both situations, which descent corporation he belongs to may partly account for his taking part, and for what he does with whom. Yet the group that joins together to fight will predictably only partly overlap with the group that sponsored the feast; and neither will correspond neatly to the group that joins together in ritual, which most nearly corresponds to "the Kwaio descent group":

> The category of persons whose primary descent affiliation is to a particular named territory (for example, "Kwangafi"), because they are agnatically descended from its founder, is relatively clear. But this category does not define a "localized descent group," since adult women are mainly scattered in their husbands' territories and some male members live in territories other than Kwangafi. "The Kwangafi people," in this neat sense of a descent category, are crystallized into a social group only in a few contexts, mainly involving ritual; they compose a dispersed ritual community, not a local group. On the other hand, in different contexts "The Kwangafi people" refers to the people domiciled in Kwangafi and their families; that is, it includes in-marrying wives not related to Kwangafi and excludes Kwangafi women living elsewhere. "The Kwangafi people" may refer also to a much wider category of all those people *cognatically* descended from the founders of Kwangafi who sacrifice to Kwangafi ancestors. In still other contexts, "The Kwangafi people" may refer to an action group temporarily crystallized around the men of Kwangafi for some purpose such as feuding or feasting; these may include a broad scattering of cognates, affines, neighbors, and political allies.
>
> . . . [T]he component elements that contribute to being a "Kwangafi person" in different contexts (descent category membership, domicile, actual residence, sex, neighborhood cluster membership, etc.) can be analytically untangled. Distinguishing the different contexts where descent status is relevant and analyzing the roles involved enables us to make sense of much of the apparent flux of social interaction. One can anticipate fairly accurately, as Kwaio can, what group or category will comprise "The Kwangafi people" in a particular setting or event (Keesing 1972:23).

Fine-grained cultural analysis of social relations underlines the inadequacy of older anthropological approaches to kinship terms. Conventionally, anthropologists have distinguished two sets of kin terms—"terms of
reference" and "terms of address." The first set is used in talking about a
relative: "He's my uncle." The second set is used in directly addressing a
relative. We know now that the anthropologist must *discover* what sets or
classes of "kin terms" are distinguished in a particular culture; there may
turn out to be one set or three. And in what social contexts and for what
social purposes these alternative sets are used must be discovered, not
assumed. In many societies, kin terms are apparently used only rarely. A
common pattern seems to be to refer to a person's kinship relation to you
not in everyday conversation, but in situations when that person is violating
the norms of kinship; or in situations when you are trying to manipulate
him (lend me a dollar, brother . . .). Use of kin terms often turns out to
be a political strategy, not an everyday social nicety. And the anthropologist
learns that only by recording social life in rich detail, and paying close
attention to roles and contexts.

Such an approach leads us to look more carefully than we usually have,
in studying tribal social organization, at the groups that form temporarily
to make gardens together, hunt together, fetch water from the stream, or
sit and gossip; and hence to give more adequate emphasis to the role of
friendship and personal choice, as well as kinship or descent status, in the
fabric of everyday social life among tribesmen. And that in turn helps us
to understand more clearly the apparent gulf between kinship ideals and
actual behavior. Kinship norms specify how people should or would behave
to one another in a world where only kinship mattered. But actual kinsmen
are also neighbors, business competitors, owners of adjacent gardens, and
so on; and their quarreling and enmity characteristically derive from these
relationships, as well as competition for inheritance, power in the family or
lineage, and so on. Brothers should support one another. But the owner of
a pig who eats your garden should pay damages. If the owner is your
brother—and in small-scale tribal societies it is your kin who will most
often be your neighbors and rivals—there is a "gulf" between the ensuing
quarrel and ideal behavior between kin. This "gulf" does not mean that the
norms or rules are wrong or unimportant; but that the world to which they
are applied is complicated and human.

Cultural analysis of social relations further suggests that the traditional
ways of looking at "a social structure" as formed from a set of corporate
descent groups articulated together into a system may be much too simple.
If we pay closer attention to who does what with whom, these neat, simple
models dissolve away. But there is then a challenge of finding deeper levels
of structure, of discovering and mapping the shared knowledge and common
code that enables native actors to maintain ordered social relations. Descent

and kinship, being central in the ideologies of so many tribal peoples, are easy to learn about and easy to diagram. But other principles, interests, and strategies may in fact be at least as central in shaping social relations—a further warning against classifying societies according to the formal features of their kinship and descent systems. Despite decades of study, anthropologists are just beginning to learn how to probe beneath the formal blueprints of social structure to understand the texture of everyday social life in other societies—or in our own.

KINSHIP AS SYMBOLIC MODEL

Cultural analysis of kinship has taken anthropologists in another somewhat different direction. Anthropologists concerned with symbolic systems—with the ways peoples conceptualize the cosmos and use key symbols as models or paradigms of their social and natural world—have increasingly been exploring the realm of kinship.

One avenue has been the work of Lévi-Strauss (1949) and subsequent theorists of alliance systems, notably Rodney Needham (1972, 1973). The way a system for the exchange of women between the alliance groups can become a model or paradigm for the whole cosmos was suggested in our example of the Purum in Chapter 5 (Case 17). A dualistic division of the social world into wife-givers and wife-takers, and male and female, can be projected onto the whole cosmos. The natural environment and the human environment—even in such realms as house-plans and language—can be conceptualized in symbolic polarities.

Another thrust of symbolic analysis of kinship has come from David Schneider (1968, 1972) and his students (e.g., Silverman 1971). Attempting to analyze cultures as symbolic systems, more or less independently of the social systems and ecological contents in which they are embedded, these scholars have seen kinship as providing primary symbols central in a people's orientation to their world. Kinship, as the preeminent relationship of natural connection and shared essence or substance—whether physical or spiritual—provides a paradigm or model of relatedness. That the biology of sex and reproduction provides a point of reference for this symbolic model should not lead us, Schneider argues (1972), into taking culturally-conceived biology as primary and the symbolic import as secondary; to understand the people we study, we must see things the other way around. (In Chapter 2, we saw an alternative view.)

A symbolic conception of kinship as a natural, inalienable connection of shared substance provides a model for close relatedness that may be used in other realms as well: to conceptualize relations with deities, in fictive (cf. "blood brothers") and adoptive kin relationship, and so on.

Taking the realm of kinship as a domain of symbolic analysis, and examining it in terms of a people's own cultural categories and assumptions, can provide crucial insights. Recall the case of the African ancestors who are conceptualized as elder elders, ever-present if invisible actors on the social scene. To view them from a Western point of view as "supernaturals" separates religion from social organization in a way that distorts peoples' world view and obscures the role relationship between living and dead kinsmen. Yet there are also dangers. One can easily be led to an excessive relativism, toward exaggerating the uniqueness of each people's cultural symbols and obscuring the important universals of human thought and experience.

Study of kinship as a symbolic order has raised the question of the relationship between kin terms and social roles. Schneider and his students have argued that kin terms are above all role-designations, and that their genealogical reference is contingent and secondary. They point to the many recorded cases where a person is classed by a kin term according to his or her role vis-à-vis ego, rather than their genealogical relationship, where the two do not coincide. Scheffler (1972) and others have countered that the genealogical usages are primary and the role-labelling by kin terms is secondary—a matter of connotation, not denotation. Since both sides in this debate agree that kin terms are sometimes used in genealogical senses, yet are sometimes used in ways appropriate to social roles that deviate from or override genealogical relatedness, the question cannot easily be resolved on empirical grounds.

In a classificatory kinship terminology, many relatives who should genealogically be classed as "grandfather" are actually roughly the age of ego's father; and some are the age of ego's siblings. Many of us have the experience of having aunts and uncles roughly our own age (or nieces and nephews roughly our own age). In a system that classes distant collaterals with lineals, the age skewing can be cumulative and drastic. If ego's FFFBSS (a member of his own patrilineage) is the same age as ego's older brother, is ego to class him as "grandfather" (appropriate on genealogical grounds) or as "older sibling" (appropriate to his role)? Ethnographers seldom tell us. In many societies, apparently it is the latter. In many other societies, including the Kwaio, classification is strictly genealogical; but then the role system and kin terms fit together only contingently and loosely. Among the Kwaio, what matters in determining appropriate role behavior is not what kin class a relative falls in, but how close or distant the relationship is.

Scholars are far from agreed on what general conclusions to draw about kin terms and social roles from the complexities and variations that are coming to light from fine-grained studies. At least it is clear that the fit between systems of linguistic labels for kinds of relatives and systems for appropriate role behavior between relatives is not the simple matter anthropologists had come to assume. One cannot list the kin terms of a culture and produce a corresponding description of social roles appropriate to each kind of relative. The complex articulation between the system of labels and the system of roles must be untangled carefully in each case.

KINSHIP IN PEASANT COMMUNITIES AND COMPLEX SOCIETIES

Anthropologists became expert at analyzing kinship by studying small-scale societies—Australian Aborigines, the Nuer, the Tallensi, the Tikopia, the Trobriand Islanders. As the tribal world has been transformed, and as anthropologists have increasingly turned attention to peasants and urbanities, new perspectives on kinship have emerged.

In complex societies, kinship characteristically remains an important basis for social cohesion and collective action. Kin groups may be significant social units in peasant communities or in the local groups—villages or castes or barrios—of complex societies. Where this is true, the kinship models derived from studying tribal societies have continued to be useful. Anthropologists have also dealt fairly successfully with *fictive* kinship, relations modelled on kinship ties. The most striking and most extensively analyzed fictive kin relations are those of *compadrazgo*, ritual co-parenthood, common in Mesoamerica and other parts of the Spanish-influenced world. A brief glance at Mexican forms of *compadrazgo* will suggest how relations modelled on those of kinship cross-cut and extend genealogical ties, and hence broaden the social horizons of individuals.

CASE 22: COMPADRAZGO IN MEXICO

Compadrazgo in Mesoamerica overtly derives from the Catholic institution of baptism: a "godfather" and "godmother" sponsor a child ritually in the baptism; they provide spiritual responsibility for the child complementary to the responsibility of father and mother for the child's physical development. While a child's relationship to *padrino* (godfather) and *madrina* (godmother) is important—marked by respect and obedience from the child and guidance and assistance from the sponsors—it is the relationship between sponsors and *parents* that has received special elaboration in Mesoamerica.

The sponsors and parents establish bonds of ritual co-parenthood which (especially between godfather and father) are important additions to kinship bonds. The reciprocal term *compadre* is used for this relationship, which characteristically has strong associations of sacredness and entails ritual respect and formalized reciprocity.

Mexican and other Latin American elaborations of *compadrazgo* have extended the range and importance of these ties far beyond the original

Catholic derivation in the sponsorship of baptism. The relationship may unite the sponsor to the grandparents, as well as parents, of the child, or otherwise extend the dyadic relationship into a multiple one. And sponsorship in other ritual events, not simply baptism, may lead an individual to have multiple ritual parents.

The variation in regional forms of *compadrazgo* presumably reflects differences in the pre-Columbian Indian cultures onto which the Spanish model has been superimposed (Davila 1971). These regional variations in the range of *compadre* relationships, their social entailments and relationships to family structure, and their function in the social life of communities have been extensively studied.

Characteristically, sponsors are non-kin or distant kin. A major function of *compadrazgo* is thus to extend the range of close dyadic relations beyond the circle of kin. In most communities, fairly free choice of a sponsor is possible. Where the social system is relatively egalitarian, the *compadre* relationship is characteristically symmetrical in terms of status. But where differences in wealth and power are marked, sponsorship by a wealthy or powerful man becomes a political strategy —a way of maintaining status (for the sponsor) and seeking upward mobility (for the son) and patronage (for the father).

The symbolic modelling of *compadrazgo* on kinship is evident not only in terminology and role relationships; but in the inalienable, enduring, sacred nature of the bonds of sponsorship and co-parenthood, the axioms of moral obligation they entail, and the extension of incest taboos to relations of *compadrazgo* (Davila 1971).

Ties of fictive kinship, or adoptive kinship, are important in many tribal societies as well (recall the so-called "parallel descent" system of the Apinayé, p. 76, where membership in ceremonial groups is based on relations with a special ceremonial "father" and "mother"). In these cases, symbolic extensions of kinship may similarly serve to broaden the range of social ties or readjust local groups according to pressures of demography and ecology.

Traditional modes of analyzing kinship have been less easily adapted to the informal networks of interpersonal relations anthropologists have encountered in large-scale societies, especially in urban settings. From social anthropologists of the British tradition, particularly those who have worked in urban African settings and in Europe, have come a series of explorations in network analysis and other modes of studying interpersonal relations. The recurrent problem, analytically, has been that corporate kin groups of the sort familiar from tribal societies are no longer in sight. Instead, each individual moves through a world without neat boundaries, interacting with friends, relatives, business associates, and others in various roles and settings. Focus on individuals making choices, forming alliances and temporary groups, advancing strategies, has been necessary. The work of such scholars as Clyde Mitchell, Elizabeth Bott, J. A. Barnes, Jeremy Boissevain, Adrian Mayer, F. G. Bailey, and Fredrik Barth has advanced our understanding of the patterning and strategy of interpersonal relationships in complex societies.

In the American tradition, explorations of the cultural knowledge underlying social relations have provided further insights. How individuals define contexts, perceive alternatives, assume appropriate roles, and make appropriate choices become crucial questions. We have barely begun to glimpse partial answers. One of the ironies of social science is that a great deal is known about the "superstructures" of society (including, in anthropology, such groupings as lineages and clans); but very little is understood about how humans perceive, act, and communicate in their everyday behavior.

The effort to interpret informal social relations in complex societies has increasingly led anthropologists to realize that the same subtleties shape social life everywhere. The seeming ease of describing tribal societies in terms of clans and lineages and kinship systems—of formal blueprints and jural rules—has been an illusion. If instead of talking about "the Nuer lineage," we ask why those three Nuer are working together over there, we find ourselves in the same position as the urban anthropologist—and in need of the same new, more powerful, ways of dealing with human complexity.

9
EVOLUTION AND ADAPTATION IN SOCIAL STRUCTURE

How the forms of social organization of the primitive world had evolved and taken shape was a prominent anthropological question in the last 30 years of the nineteenth century. Lewis Henry Morgan, pioneer in the comparative study of kinship terminologies, sought to read into these terminologies evidence about the evolutionary stages through which primitive peoples had passed. For others, such as Westermarck, tidbits of titillating evidence about bizarre marriage customs and the like were used to construct hypothetical and fanciful evolutionary schemes.

The foundations for more sound comparative study were laid by Sir Edward Tylor, in a famous 1889 paper in which he proposed that statistical associations between forms of marriage and kin grouping from different parts of the tribal world could reveal the functional relationships between elements of these complexes and make possible sound reconstruction of how they developed (Tylor 1889).

The two major thrusts toward modern interpretations of how forms of social structure fit together and develop came after a 25 year period (roughly 1915–1940) when "conjectural history" was in disrepute—when the functional interconnectedness of kinship systems, but not their development, had commanded attention. The first was the work, led by G. P. Murdock, of systematically building up comparative files of cross-cultural evidence to permit systematic exploration of Tylor's seminal ideas. The second was the revival of concern with cultural evolution, and a concomitant concern with ecological adaptation, pioneered by Leslie White and Julian Steward. Most modern interpretations of the evolution and adaptation of kin groups and kinship systems represent some synthesis of these enterprises.

To create such a synthesis, based on broad cross-cultural evidence systematically compared, demands first of all a framework of classification. Here Murdock has been the pioneer and leader. Inevitably, classifying descent systems, or marriage rules, or residence rules, or kinship terms involves some distortion, since the uniqueness of individual cultures is to some extent forced into a standard mold. Classifying residence rules, for example, is not the simple and straightforward business we once hoped (Goodenough 1956). And the categories used have too often been defective (e.g., Murdock classes Dravidian and Iroquois kinship terminologies together as "bifurcate-merging," though their structural entailments are very different). But in general, Murdock's classification schemes have undergone progressive refinements, from the 1949 sample used in *Social Structure* to the *Ethnographic Atlas* of twenty years later, geared for computer analysis (Murdock 1967).

Armed with large worldwide samples that show how kinds of kin groups are statistically associated with modes of subsistence and settlement patterns, for example, we can begin to assess carefully the relationship between social structure and ecology. Some sample statistics are suggestive here (based on Aberle's 1961 analysis of Murdock's 1957 sample) (Table 8).

The association between matrilineal descent, agricultural subsistence, a division of labor where women are important, and sedentary residence is fairly clear (Aberle 1961). Patrilineal descent is clearly more common and seemingly adaptive to a wider range of ecological circumstances.

Nineteenth century cultural evolutionists had mainly seen matrilineal descent as a very old pattern. Primitive promiscuity of a protohuman society had, according to speculation, given way to systems where, in ignorance of physical paternity but visibly confronted with maternity, primordial savages reckoned connection through the mother—leading to matriliny. From that state of ignorance rose the male-dominated patrilineal conditions the Victorian male found more reassuring.

It is clear from the comparative evidence that matrilineal *descent systems* are a recent and specialized development, not an ancient and primitive form. As we have seen, what we are learning about human evolution makes the Victorian imaginings almost certainly wrong. Cultural recognition of physical paternity may be comparatively recent, perhaps even within the last 50,000 years. But by this time, the basic structure of the early human family—with pair-bonding between male and female, a nuclear family, and probably intermarriage between bands and avoidance of incest (by practice if not necessarily by rule)—had very probably been long established.

TABLE 8

Descent and Subsistence Modes. Percentages show proportion within each column (e.g., percent of total matrilineal descent systems associated with dominant horticulture).

SUBSISTENCE TYPE	DESCENT SYSTEM									
	Patrilineal		Bilateral*		Matrilineal		Duolineal**		Total	
	No.	%	No.	%	No.	%	No.	%	No.	%
Plough agriculture	69	28	38	19	9	11	1	4	117	21
African horticulture (large domestic animals)	32	13	3	2	5	6	6	21	46	8
Dominant horticulture	66	27	68	33	47	56	7	25	188	33
Other horticulture	11	4	15	7	5	6	2	7	33	6
Pastoralists	51	21	8	4	3	4	4	14	66	12
New World pastoralists	0	0	11	5	2	2	0	0	13	2
Hunting and gathering/ fishing	19	8	61	30	13	16	8	29	101	18
TOTAL	248	101	204	100	84	101	28	100	564	100

* Includes a range of bilateral and cognatic forms of organization.
** Includes double descent systems and Australian section systems.

Even the late Australopithecines of two million years ago, and almost certainly *Homo erectus* of half a million years ago, were probably well on their way to a human-like family. What happened within the last 100,000 years, with increases in brainpower and the ability to make speech sounds, was the comparatively rapid elaboration of symbolic systems, including language in its modern forms. Early humans, in weaving conceptions of kinship and marriage, were almost certainly reinforcing with cultural symbols patterns that they and even their quite distant ancestors had evolved. Early savages living in primitive promiscuity, or in ignorance of paternity due to random mating, are figments of faulty inference as well as overly vivid imagination.

Matrilineal descent systems, far from being ancient, are very recent in terms of the long sweep of human development. They probably have developed within the last 5000 years, since it is within that period that the major development and spread of agricultural complexes (maize in the Americas, yams and taro in the Pacific, root crops in Africa) in the tribal world occurred.

Patrilineal descent reckoning, as noted in Chapter 1, can develop rather simply as an ideological elaboration of statistical patterns apparently common among Paleolithic hunter-gatherers. That is, a band organization where women marry out and men remain produces a *de facto* alignment of men-related-through-men. Among Australian Aborigines, a kind of supernaturally mediated descent reckoning occurred with hunters-gatherers (though at this ecological level, primacy of the nuclear family and bilateral kinship reckoning are frequent organizational themes).

The dominant theory of how patrilineal descent groups arose sees divisions of labor in which men play the major part (herding, some agricultural systems) plus the development of property as crucial formative factors. Male dominance in subsistence will make a pattern of virilocal residence adaptive, hence will result in the coresidence of men related through their fathers (and cumulatively, by chains of patrilineal connection). The development of property—whether in the form of land, cattle, horses, tents, or even grazing territory—can make some kind of corporate exercise of title adaptive. Moreover, the solidarity of patrilineally formed groups, hence their collective and corporate action, was undoubtedly often reinforced by warfare and feuding. As we saw with the Nuer (Case 7), segmentary descent connections between local corporations would apparently also be highly adaptive in producing larger alliances when needed to fight for survival or resources.

This, in the case of patrilineal descent, demands no great stretches of the imagination. It fits well what we know about tribal societies and hunting-gathering people of the ethnographic present. Since virilocal residence is a preponderant pattern worldwide, and since except in very rare cases (e.g., the Shavante, Case 6) patrilineal descent groupings are accompanied by virilocal residence, this interpretation of how they formed seems solidly supported.

Note carefully the postulated sequence that leads to *changes* in the form of kin groups: a shift in technology, or a change in environment, makes a change in the division of labor appropriate; the balance in those subsistence tasks performed by men and women changes. If the balance shifts in a direction that makes the existing pattern of postmarital residence maladaptive, the statistical frequency of residence choices shifts and eventually the ideological "rules" are changed. The changed pattern of residence then shifts the composition of local groups. As the composition of local groups stabilizes into a new pattern, that pattern can be recognized ideologically by a changed rule of descent or conceptualization of kin groups. Murdock (1949, 1959) who most clearly articulated this interpretation of the process of change (drawing on insights of Tylor, Lowie, and others), saw social structures as more or less stable, and more or less well integrated, depending on whether the full sequence of adjustments resulting from a shift in residence rules has been worked out. The adjustments to a new pattern of local group membership include changes in kinship terminology and rules for kin behavior; but these may lag behind (cf. Barnes 1971b).

This sequence is used to explain the development and evolution of matrilineal descent systems. Matrilineal descent, according to this interpretation, is triggered by a change in the division of labor (of a sedentary agricultural people) that enhances the role of women in subsistence. This promotes a statistical shift toward uxorilocal residence; and this, in turn, promotes the formation of local groups in which women related through women predominate; their husbands are outsiders. It promotes the formation of matrilineally related extended family households. The local group, with increasingly corporate rights over land, comes to be conceptualized in terms of matrilineal descent. If this process continued, a Crow kinship terminology would be a probable outcome, though an Iroquois terminology is possible.

A subsequent shift in the division of labor may lead to a shift to viriavunculocal residence, as in the Trobriands, with the matrilineal descent groups remaining strong. But a strong shift toward male dominance in the division of labor is likely to result in a shift to viri-patrilocal residence, where the matrilineages then no longer are localized and their importance declines. Eventually, matrilineal descent groups disappear and patrilineal ones are likely to develop in their place, corresponding to the changed composition of local groups (Gough 1961). Note that less than half of the matrilineal descent systems recorded have uxorilocal residence as the common form (Table 9).

Such a notion of "lag" in the readjustment of social structure to changed conditions is used to explain the widespread occurrence of a descent system with the "wrong" residence rule, a kinship terminology with the "wrong" marriage system or descent rule, and so on. We are supposed to have faith that these are due to delays in the adjustment process that in the long run would produce integrated and internally consistent social structure.

Murdock's massive reconstruction of the worldwide evolution of kinships systems (1949) rested on statistical patterns of covariation. Critics were quick to point out that when custom X is commonly correlated with custom Y, it cannot comfortably be concluded that X "causes" Y or that Y "causes" X. They may both in fact be a result of Z, which got left out. Driver (1966), in a sophisticated analysis of North America, tried to test Murdock's general model by showing statistically that changes took place in the postulated order. But the plausibility of the scheme depends in large measure on one's willingness to accept the notion of lag in the adjustment process to account for such phenomena as matrilineal descent and virilocal residence, or a Crow terminology with patrilineages.

From the direction of cultural ecology and cultural evolutionism were

TABLE 9

Residence Rules in Matrilineal Descent Systems. (Aberle 1961, based on Murdock's 1957 sample.) (Originally published by the University of California Press; reprinted by permission of The Regents of the University of California.)

RESIDENCE RULE	FREQUENCY	%
Uxorilocal and Dominantly Uxorilocal	41	49
Viri-avunculocal and Dominantly Viri-avunculocal	22	27
Dominantly Duolocal*	3	4
Dominantly Viri-Patrilocal	15	18
Dominantly Neolocal and Bilocal	3	4
TOTAL	84	102

* Residence in two different locations (as in the alternating residence of the Dobuans (p. 71).

coming slightly different perspectives. Steward (1955) had postulated that there is a "core" area of culture that is particularly responsive to ecological adaptation: the division of labor; the size and stability of local groups and their distribution in space; and residence rules. Adjustments to ecological pressures directly affected these core elements of social structure; thus, the seasonality of climate, availability of water supplies, or fertility of the soil would shape how many people could live in settlements, how permanent these could be, how they would be scattered, and how the population would organize their productive efforts. These influences on social structure then ramified through a culture so as to promote changes in realms only secondarily related to ecology—cosmological ideas, patterns of political succession, art, and the like.

Meanwhile, Leslie White (1959) and his students had sought to work out worldwide evolutionary sequences whereby advances in technology (measured in terms of thermodynamic efficiency in the subsistence return of energy expended) enabled progressively larger, more complex, and differentiated organizations of society. Elman Service's evolutionary interpretation of social organization, positing a series of organizational stages (bands, tribes, chiefdoms . . .), represents a major comparative synthesis. Unfortunately, such a scheme badly oversimplifies the evidence so as to fit the comparative data into evolutionary stages. For example, "patrilocal bands" are viewed as the standard form of hunter-gatherer social organization; yet as we saw in Chapter 1, modern field studies are revealing much more diverse and flexible forms of local group organization among hunter-gatherers. Service explains such forms as anomalies resulting from the modern contact situation. In dealing with tribal societies, Service views unilineal descent groupings as the standard evolutionary adaptation among food-producers without centralized political systems. Yet as we have seen, cognatic and bilateral systems occur in a substantial proportion of these societies; and they cannot be dismissed, as Service is inclined to do, as products of European disruption. Such worldwide evolutionary schemes fit the comparative facts less and less well, and their influence has receded in recent years.

Sahlins' (1960) suggestion that such schemes of worldwide cultural evolution in technology be distinguished from detailed study of the "adaptive radiation" of societies into diverse environmental niches gave a further push toward careful study of cultures as adaptive systems. We have noted Sahlins' interpretation of the segmentary lineage systems of the Tiv and Nuer as adaptations to "predatory expansion" (see Chapter 3 and Sahlins 1961); and his ecological interpretation of the contrast between ramifying and descent-line systems in Polynesia (see Chapter 3 and Sahlins 1958). Murdock's interpretations had used ecology as a kind of prime mover; and a greater concern with cultural ecology and adaptation has characterized most subsequent theories of the development of kinship systems. Predictably, when anthropologists first got around to sorting out cognatic descent systems and bilaterally organized societies, they sought ecological interpretations for their development.

Thus Goodenough (1955) offered a provocative interpretation of how the speakers of Malayo-Polynesian languages in the island Pacific (Melanesians, Micronesians, and Polynesians) might have developed patrilineal, matrilineal, and cognatic descent systems in different areas. If the ancestral system was based on a reckoning of cognatic descent, but had a rule of postmarital residence such that the couple could opt to live either with the husband's kin (virilocally) or the wife's kin (uxorilocally), with the children then belonging either to husband's or wife's descent group respectively (recall the Iban *bilek*, Case 21), a number of possibilities would follow. Where land resources were scarce and likely to get out of balance with descent group membership (as on small Pacific atolls), such a rule of descent and residence would seem highly flexible and adaptive. If husband's group were short of land, and wife's group had an abundance of land, the couple would be likely to opt to live where they could get more land. The children would then belong to the group with greater land, thus redistributing population by a kind of cybernetic process so that optimum resource use would be possible. Such an ancestral system could easily develop into the various cognatic descent forms found in the Pacific. But where ecological conditions favored an increased importance of women in subsistence tasks, a statistical shift to uxorilocal residence could easily lead to matrilineal descent systems. Conversely, where an increased subsistence role of men was adaptive, the ancestral cognatic system could easily shift into a patrilineal descent system.

Goodenough's hypothesis has been challenged by a number of specialists on the New Guinea highlands, who have pointed out that among such people as the Chimbu (Case 10), cognatic affiliations do not increase as population density increases and land becomes scarce. Rather, the patrilineal dogma hardens, and nonagnates are denied use of land they would have been allowed to use when resources were abundant. But it is not clear that the systems, or situations, are directly comparable.

Later, Goodenough (1962) sought to account for a pattern of shifting settlement and cognatic kin groups among the Lakalai of New Britain as a consequence of an environment where destructive earthquakes were common and had forced frequent regrouping of refugee groups. While this may be reasonable in the Lakalai case, it does not get one very far as a general explanation of the complex mosaic of different forms of kin group in Melanesia: Hogbin (1963) rejects it as a "just-so story." The diversity, but also the recurrence of similar forms, found in Melanesia show vividly the challenge to anthropological explanation and the inadequacy of our present explanatory means. An example from the Solomon Islands will illustrate. Scheffler (1965) has described a cognatic descent system from Choiseul Island (Figure 42) that is strikingly similar in its formal outlines to the system of the Kwaio described in Case 16, and other peoples of Malaita. The parallels are as specific as this: the Choiseul term for a nonagnatic affiliant to a kin group is literally "born of women"; an agnate is "born of men." In Kwaio, the words themselves used for nonagnates and agnates are completely unrelated, but literally translate as "born of women" and "born of men." That the words of the Choiseulese and Kwaio are different is not surprising. The languages are less closely related historically than English and Persian (Farsi). The Kaoka speakers of Guadalcanal are close cultural relatives of the Kwaio, and speak a closely related language. In religion and economics, and political leadership the Kaoka and Malaitans are very similar; their kin terms are virtually the same as those of Malaita (Hogbin 1964). There are no sharp contrasts in ecological adaptation. Yet the Kaoka are organized in matrilineal descent groups (as are the other close cultural relatives of Malaitans, on San Cristobal), where the Malaitans all have patrilineal or cognatic descent groups (see Figure 42).

What accounts for the sharp differences between the Malaitans and their matrilineally-organized cultural relatives? What accounts for the striking formal similarities between the Malaitans and the historically unrelated peoples of Choiseul? Perhaps it has something to do with an apparently greater reliance in Malaita and Choiseul on taro, a root vegetable that is harvested and replanted continuously year-round; and the greater reliance

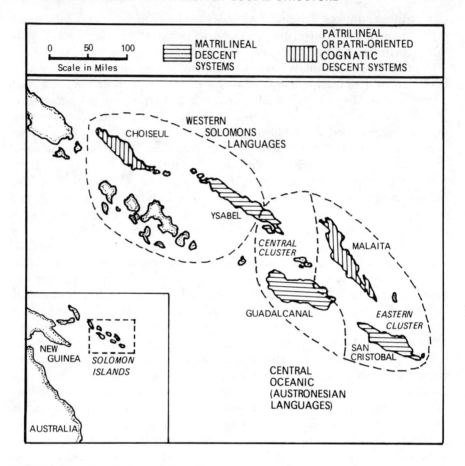

FIGURE 42 The Solomon Islands: Social Organization and Language. The Western Solomons languages, though classed by specialists as a branch of Austronesian, are more distantly related to the Central Oceanic Austronesian languages than the latter are to the languages of Indonesia and the Philippines.

in Guadalcanal on yams, which are planted seasonally and stored. But this is only a matter of degree and emphasis, and the ecological contrasts seem slight. We are left groping for an explanation.

That partly reflects the poverty of our theoretical resources. Ecological adaptation is undoubtedly important in shaping kin-group organization; but it probably shapes and prunes indirectly rather than directly, neatly, and consistently. The role of ideology has often been underestimated by those who stress the adaptiveness of social forms. Moreover, the dynamics of change are often lost sight of if we see ecological pressures as operating directly and mechanically on cultural systems. Cultures do not respond to pressures. Rather, individual human beings cope as best they can, formulate rules, follow and break them; and by their statistical patterns of cumulative decisions, they set a course of cultural drift.

In this process, the effect of ecological forces has often been conceived too mechanically. We need a theory of change in social structure that takes into account both the clear importance of ecological adaptation and the importance of humans as creators and manipulators of rules. Perspectives derived from Marxist theory have given a major new impetus to anthropological understanding of social change. Marxist-derived models see the relationship between the technology of production and the social organization of production not as mechanical, but dialectical. Social relations are not automatically adjusted in an ecologically adaptive way to changes in technology. Rather, a process of mutual adjustment, in both directions, between technology and social organization—control over the means of production, the division of labor, the size and composition of work groups— generates progressive changes. Moreover, Marxist-influenced models illuminate the connections between control over the means of production, political power, and ideologies about the social order. Ideologies are seen not simply as secondary by-products of ecological adaptation, as some "cultural materialists" (notably Marvin Harris [1968]) would imply, but as dynamic forces in the process of change.

An effective synthesis of Marxist-derived and ecological-adaptationist models of change, facilitated by the formal models of cybernetics and systems theory, seems within reach. Marxist models of the "lineage mode of production" advanced by such scholars as Terray (1972) are still too simplistic; and systems-theoretic ecological models advanced by such scholars as Rappaport (1971) are still too closed and equilibrium-bound. But recent work by Talal Asad (1972) and others, where the relations between control over resources, power, and ecology are traced, suggests that a meeting in the middle—or above and beyond—may be close at hand.

Where unequal access to resources and control over surpluses have developed into a hierarchical system of social classes (as Asad argues is the case for the Swat Pathans of Northern Pakistan, and as is clearly the case for Tonga [Case 9], Bunyoro [Case 8], and many other anthropologically-studied societies), the bases for contradiction, polarization, exploitation, and either a progressive widening of the gulf between classes or class struggle and upheaval, are fairly clear. When productive labor and control over resources and surpluses are divorced, hierarchies of domination clearly contain the seeds of their own transformation (in whatever direction).

But the case is less clear for societies where marked social classes are absent and where producers control resources and subsist on the fruits of their own labor—"the lineage mode of production" in its variant forms. Yet in such societies, where marked social classes are absent, a series of "battle lines" still exist along which social changes may be advanced, and which are continuously being fought or renegotiated.

1. The balance of power between the sexes. The relative power and status of men and women, as represented in their role in production and their control over resources and means of production (including technical and ritual knowledge); and as represented in residence rules, property rights, rules of descent, ritual participation, rules of sexual conduct, and so on.
2. The balance of power between old and young, or between the young, the parental generation, and the grandparental generation. Control over sacred knowledge and "wisdom" may give elders powers, including those of warfare. Older and younger are likely to have conflicting rights and interests with regard to political and economic power, access to women, and so on; but in some contexts, elders and juniors may have common interests vis-à-vis mature adults.
3. The common interests of age-mates in different kin groups versus the common interests of members of the same kin-based corporations (vis-à-vis outsiders).
4. The relative strength of ties between husband-and-wife and between brother-and-sister.
5. The opposition and conflict of descent or territorial groups over access to resources (land, women, property, prestige) versus their unity for common goals (place, collective security, joint enterprise).
6. The relative importance of collective rights and individual rights (as in the unity of brothers in corporate action versus their rivalry and separation, and in the unity of lineage corporations versus kinship ties outside the lineage).

Such boundaries of rights, duties, and authority are in this view continually open to negotiation—with rules being created, broken, redefined, and elaborated. Shifts in the ecological balance may enhance the bargaining power of men or women, increase the self-sufficiency of spouse-pairs, and so on; and it is cumulative individual deviations from a rule or norm that make possible the assertion of a new one. But changes in the rules are not simply *produced by* changes in ecology or in the statistical patterns of individual action. Rules are at once statements and metaphors about the state of the battle lines, challenges against previous rules, and targets for renegotiation. And violations and deviations from public norms are also, in a sense, assertions of new ones.

Such a model serves to remind us—if we need reminding despite the women's movement—that "egalitarian societies" are usually egalitarian from the point of view of adult men. It further underlines the tenuous balance of egalitarianism. The internal dynamics of societies, fed by conflict and contradiction as ecological circumstances and technology permit the accumulation of surpluses and control of crucial scarce goods, can lead easily in the direction of class differentiation. In some New Guinea highlands societies and the Trobriand Islands (Case 13), where groups much larger than those characteristic of Melanesia were concentrated, incipient class systems were developing out of the "Big Man" system. In traditional Melanesian societies, feast-giving and exchange enabled a successful leader to acquire power and influence over a cluster of supporters; but this influence was contingent on continuing success, and was not hereditary. Yet in some ecologically favored areas, the gulf between leaders controlling elaborate exchange systems and their followers and supporters seems to have been widening. Perhaps, had European intrusion come a century later, some Melanesian political systems would have been more like the Polynesian systems of Tonga (Case 9) and New Zealand (Case 19) than those of their less-ecologically-favored cultural cousins.

We may also need a Lévi-Straussian corollary to Parkinson's Law[1]: that the human mind expands and elaborates cultural detail to fill whatever "space" is available. This space may be produced by a freedom from ecological pressure (as on the northwest coast of North America), a freedom from material encumbrances (as in Australia), a seasonable cycle that provides a time of plenty and communal action, and so on. Or it may result from shifts in the "battle lines," where men acquire great strength vis-à-vis women, age-mates attain power vis-à-vis kin groups, and so on.

If this view is correct, the relationship between social structure and environment is indirect, mediated by ideologies and the dynamics of "negotiation"—so our search for perfect correlations of what-goes-with-what-under-what-conditions may be doomed to failure. But it enables us to break away from equilibrium models and views of social structures as frozen that hamper our understanding of change; and it connects the abstract formal structure of "the system" with the dynamics of social process and of individual psychology.

[1] "Work expands to fill the time available for its completion" (Parkinson 1957).

GLOSSARY

GLOSSARY

AFFINE A relative by marriage. (Normally, however, the spouse of a parent's sibling and reciprocally, the child of one's spouse's sibling, are classed with consanguineal relatives, not affines.)

AFFINITY Relationship by marriage. May include the relationship between corporate groups linked by marriage between their members.

AGNATE A person related by patrilineal descent.

AGNATIC (DESCENT) *see* PATRILINEAL.

ALLIANCE A system whereby descent groups or other kin groups are linked by a rule of prescriptive or recurrent marriage so that the groups remain in an affinal relationship to one another across generations.

APICAL ANCESTOR (ANCESTRESS) The ancestor or ancestress from which descent is traced (the "apex" of the triangle of descendants).

ASYMMETRICAL ALLIANCE In alliance theory, a marriage system involving indirect exchange. (Patrilateral alliance is considered by some theorists to be nonexistent or impossible, so matrilateral alliance—marriage with MBD or a girl classed with her—is the form commonly referred to as asymmetrical.)

AVUNCULOCAL (Postmarital) residence of a person with mother's brother. (Since characteristically this entails residence of a couple with the *husband's* maternal uncle, the terms *viri-avunculocal* or *avuncu-virilocal* are more precise.)

BILATERAL (KINSHIP) Kinship traced to relatives through both father and mother (syn. "consanguineal kinship").

BRIDE PRICE *see* BRIDEWEALTH.

BRIDEWEALTH Marriage payments from the husband and his kin to the bride's kin. Characteristically these payments balance a transfer of rights over the wife's sexuality, work services, residence, fertility, and so on.

CLAN A unilineal descent group or category whose members trace patrilineal descent (patriclan) or matrilineal descent (matriclan) from an apical ancestor/ancestress, but do not know the genealogical links that connect them to this apical ancestor.

CLASSIFICATORY SYSTEM A mode of kinship classification in which collateral kin are terminologically equated with lineal kin (FB = F, MZ = M, etc.).

COGNATE A bilateral (consanguineal) kinsman or kinswoman.

COGNATIC (DESCENT) *Sense 1:* A mode of descent reckoning where all descendants of an apical ancestor/ancestress through any combination of male or female links are included (preferred sense). *Sense 2:* Synonymous with *bilateral* or *consanguineal* (*see* BILATERAL, CONSANGUINEAL) as in "cognatic kinship" (syn. "bilateral kinship").

COLLATERAL In kinship terminologies, the siblings of lineal relatives (parents, grandparents) and their descendants.

COMPLEMENTARY FILIATION In the work of Fortes, Goody, and others, the relationship between a person and his/her maternal uncle and his lineage (in a patrilineal descent system); or between a person and his/her paternal aunt/uncle and their lineage (in a matrilineal descent system).

CONSANGUINEAL A relative by birth (i.e., a "blood" relative), as distinguished from in-laws ("affines") and step-relatives.

CORPORATE GROUP A social group whose members act as a legal individual in terms of collective rights to property, a common group name, collective responsibility, and so on.

CROSS-COUSIN A cousin related to ego through ego's mother's brother or ego's father's sister (i.e., cross-cousins are the children of a brother and sister).

CROSS-COUSIN MARRIAGE In alliance theory (especially in its early versions), a rule or practice of marriage between father's sister's child and mother's brother's child (a man's marriage with MBD is "matrilateral," with FZD is "patrilateral").

CROW TERMINOLOGY A mode of kinship classification usually but not always associated with matrilineal descent in which a line of father's matrilineal kin are terminologically equated across generations (mirror image of Omaha terminology).

DESCENT A relationship defined by connection to an ancestor (or ancestress) through a culturally recognized sequence of parent-child links (from father to son to son's son = patrilineal descent, from mother to daughter to daughter's daughter = matrilineal descent).

DESCENT GROUP A kin group whose membership is based on a rule of descent. Appropriate descent status (patrilineal, matrilineal, or cognatic, depending on the society) entitles a person to be a member of the group.

DESCENT RULE A descent principle culturally used to define eligibility for membership in a kin group.

DIRECT EXCHANGE (*échange restreint*) A system of alliance (prescriptive marriage) whereby kin groups exchange wives directly (so that wife-givers are the same people as wife-takers).

DOMESTIC GROUP A social group occupying or centered in a dwelling house, living (and usually eating) together, and characteristically exercising corporate control over family property.

DOUBLE DESCENT A system whereby two sets of social groups or categories exist (for different purposes) in the same society, one based on patrilineal descent and the other on matrilineal descent (so a person belongs to his/ her father's patrilineal group and his/her mother's matrilineal group).

DOWRY Goods sent with a girl at her marriage, either as (political) payment to the husband's kin or (more commonly) as payment of the woman's share of her family estate.

DRAVIDIAN TERMINOLOGY A mode of kinship reckoning whereby parallel and cross relatives (or "kin" and "affines") are systematically distinguished; characteristically, but apparently not always, associated with a rule of symmetrical alliance (direct exchange), i.e., a two-section system.

ENDOGAMY A requirement for marriage within a defined category or range or group or community ("in-marriage"). All societies are minimally endogamous in that they limit marriage to members of the same species; most limit marriage to members of the opposite sex.

EXOGAMY A requirement for marriage outside a particular social group or range of kinship.

EXTENDED FAMILY A domestic group or composite of domestic groups consisting of two or more nuclear families linked together through parent and child (patrilineal extended family, matrilineal extended family) or through siblings (fraternal or sororal extended family).

FICTIVE KINSHIP A relationship, such as godparenthood, modelled on relations of kinship, but created by customary convention rather than the circumstances of birth.

FILIATION Relationship to or through one's father and one's mother, or the basing of rights on this relationship.

HAWAIIAN KINSHIP TERMINOLOGY A mode of kinship reckoning, usually associated with bilateral kinship or cognatic descent, in which relatives are distinguished only according to sex and generation.

INCEST TABOO A rule prohibiting sexual relations between immediate kin (father and daughter, mother and son, brother and sister) and others culturally defined as in an equivalent relationship. Differs from *exogamy*, which prohibits marriage but not necessarily sexual relations.

INDIRECT EXCHANGE (*échange géneralisé*) A system of alliance (prescriptive marriage) whereby kin groups exchange wives indirectly, so that a man must marry his actual or classificatory MBD (matrilineal alliance) or FZD (patrilineal alliance, said not to exist) but so that wife-givers cannot be wife-takers.

IROQUOIS TERMINOLOGY A mode of kinship reckoning, usually but not always associated with unilineal descent, in which cross and parallel relatives are distinguished according to relative sex of connecting relatives in the middle three generations only.

JOINT FAMILY *see* EXTENDED FAMILY.

KIN GROUP A social group whose members define their relationship (or their eligibility for membership) on kinship or common descent.

KINDRED A social group or category consisting of an individual's circle of relatives, or that range of a person's relatives accorded special cultural recognition.

KINSHIP Relationship based on or modeled on the culturally recognized connection between parents and children (and extended to siblings and through parents to more distant relatives).

KINSHIP TERMINOLOGY A system of linguistic categories for denoting kinds of relatives.

LEVIRATE A system where a dead man's brother (or equivalent close male relative) succeeds to his status as husband, by marrying his widow.

LINEAGE A unilineal descent group based on patrilineal descent (patrilineage) or matrilineal descent (matrilineage) whose members trace descent from an apical ancestor/ancestress by known genealogical links.

MATRILATERAL Based on relationship on the mother's side.

MATRILINEAGE *see* LINEAGE.

MATRILINEAL A principle of descent from an ancestress through her daughter, her daughter's daughter, and so on (in the female line).

MATRILOCAL *see* UXORILOCAL.

MOIETY A division of a society into two social categories or groups, characteristically by a rule of patrilineal descent (patri-moiety) or matrilineal descent (matri-moiety).

NEOLOCAL Residence of a couple after marriage in a new household not linked spatially to that of the groom's or the bride's kin (cf. virilocal, uxorilocal).

NONUNILINEAL DESCENT An alternative term to "cognatic descent." Since cognatic descendants *include* patrilineal descendants and matrilineal descendants this usage is unfortunate. I have suggested that the term be used in societies that recognize a unilineal core within a cognatic descent category to denote descent status through at least one alternate-sex link (i.e., nonagnatic where descent includes at least one female link, nonuterine where it includes at least one male link).

NUCLEAR FAMILY A family unit consisting of parents and their dependent children.

OMAHA TERMINOLOGY A mode of kinship classification usually but not always associated with patrilineal descent in which a line of mother's patrilineal kin are terminologically equated across generations (mirror image of Crow terminologies).

PARALLEL COUSIN Ego's father's brother's child or mother's sister's child, or more distant cousin classed terminologically with these first cousins.

PATRILATERAL Based on relationship through the father's side.

PATRILINEAGE *see* LINEAGE.

PATRILINEAL DESCENT Descent traced through a line of ancestors in the male line (syn. AGNATIC DESCENT).

PATRILOCAL *see* VIRILOCAL.

PERSONAL KINDRED *see* KINDRED.

PHRATRY A grouping of clans related by traditions of common descent or historical alliance based on kinship.

POLYANDRY Marriage of a woman to two or more men.

POLYGYNY Marriage of a man to two or more women.

PREFERENTIAL Of a marriage pattern (e.g., marriage with a cross-cousin, a brother's widow, etc.), socially valued and desirable, but not enjoined.

PRESCRIPTIVE MARRIAGE In alliance theory, a requirement that marriage be with a partner in a particular kinship category. Even where "incorrect" marriages occur, they are likely to be classed as if they were correct, and kinship relations readjusted accordingly.

RAMAGE A term used by Firth to denote a cognatic descent group; and by Sahlins, to denote a descent system where local descent groups are ranked according to seniority of descent, as in Tonga.

RELATIONSHIP SYSTEMS Term used by Needham and other proponents of the "category" approach to kinship terms to denote "kinship" terminologies (this avoids the genealogical implication).

RESIDENCE RULES Conventions for residence by a couple after marriage, defining whether they reside with husband's kin, wife's kin, or others.

SECTION SYSTEM In alliance theory and Australian kinship studies, division of a society into two, four, or eight social categories through rules of descent and alliance. Symmetrical rules of marital alliance, enjoining marriage with a member of one of the sections, are a normal accompaniment of such systems.

SEGMENTARY Of descent systems, defining descent categories with reference to more and more remote apical ancestors so that the descent categories form a tree-like structure (including successively wider ranges of descendants).

SISTER-EXCHANGE Exchange of sisters in marriage by a pair of men.

SORORATE A form of secondary marriage whereby, upon the death of a wife, her sister or some other close relative marries the surviving husband. This perpetuates the marital contract between groups.

SYMMETRICAL ALLIANCE In alliance theory, a marriage system involving direct exchange. *See* DIRECT EXCHANGE.

TOTEMISM Symbolic association between a social group (e.g., a lineage or clan) and a kind of bird, plant, or natural phenomenon. In "classic" forms, a member of the social group has some special religious relationship (e.g., a food taboo) toward members of the natural species.

UNILINEAL Patrilineal (agnatic) or matrilineal (uterine) descent.

UTERINE *see* MATRILINEAL.

UXORILOCAL Residence of a married couple with the wife's kin (formerly called "matrilocal").

VIRILOCAL Residence of a married couple with the husband's kin (formerly called "patrilocal"). Residence rules can be further distinguished as viri-patrilocal (with the husband's father—patri-virilocal expresses the same pattern), viri-avunculocal (or avunculo-virilocal)—residence with the husband's maternal uncle.

REFERENCES

REFERENCES

ABERLE, D. F. 1961 "Matrilineal Descent in Cross-Cultural Perspective," in D. Schneider and K. Gough, eds., *Matrilineal Kinship*. Berkeley: University of California Press.

ASAD, T. 1972 "Market Model, Class Structure and Consent: A Reconsideration of Swat Political Organization," *Man* (n.s.), 7:74–94.

AYOUB, M. 1959 "Parallel Cousin Marriage and Endogamy," *Southwestern Journal of Anthropology*, 15:226–275.

BAILEY, F. G. 1971 *Gifts and Poison*. Oxford, England: Blackwell.

BARNES, J. A. 1962 "African Models in the New Guinea Highlands," *Man*, 62:5–9.

———. 1967a *Inquest on the Murngin*. Royal Anthropological Institute of Great Britain and Ireland. Occasional Paper No. 26.

———. 1967b "Genealogies," in A. L. Epstein, ed., *The Craft of Social Anthropology*. London: Tavistock.

———. 1971a *Social Networks*. Addison-Wesley Modules in Anthropology. Reading, Mass.: Addison-Wesley.

———. 1971b *Three Styles in the Study of Kinship*. London: Tavistock.

BARTH, F. 1966 *Models of Social Organization*. Royal Anthropological Institute. Occasional Paper No. 23. London: Royal Anthropological Institute.

BEATTIE, J. 1958 *Nyoro Kinship, Marriage, and Affinity*. London: Oxford University Press.

———. 1960 *The Bunyoro: An African Kingdom*. New York: Holt, Rinehart and Winston, Inc.

——. 1964 "Kinship and Social Anthropology," *Man*, 64:101–103.

BICCHIERI, M. 1972 *Hunters and Gatherers Today.* New York: Holt, Rinehart and Winston, Inc.

BIGGS, B. 1960 *Maori Marriage.* Polynesian Society Maori Monograph No. 1. Wellington, New Zealand.

BOHANNAN, P. 1954a *Tiv Farm and Settlement.* London: H. M. Stationery Office.

——. 1954b "The Migration and Expansion of the Tiv," *Africa*, 24:2–16.

BOHANNAN, P., AND L. BOHANNAN. 1968 *Tiv Economy.* Evanston, Ill.: Northwestern University Press.

BOHANNAN, P., AND J. MIDDLETON, eds. 1968a *Kinship and Social Organization.* New York: Natural History Press.

——. 1968b *Marriage, Family and Residence.* New York: Natural History Press.

BOISSEVAIN, J. 1968 "The Place of Non-Groups in the Social Sciences," *Man* (n.s.), 3:542–556.

BOTT, E. 1971 *Family and Social Networks.* 2d ed. London: Tavistock.

BROOKFIELD, H. C., AND P. BROWN 1963 *Struggle for Land: Agriculture and Group Territories among the Chimbu of the New Guinea Highlands.* Melbourne: Oxford University Press.

BROWN, P. 1962 "Non-Agnates among the Patrilineal Chimbu," *Journal of the Polynesian Society*, 71:57–64.

——. 1967 "The Chimbu Political System," *Anthropological Forum*, 2:36–52.

——. 1972 *The Chimbu: A Study of Change in the New Guinea Highlands.* Cambridge, Mass.: Schenkman.

BUCHLER, I. R., AND H. A. SELBY 1968 *Kinship and Social Organization: An Introduction to Theory and Method.* New York: Macmillan.

COLSON, E. 1958 *Marriage and the Family among the Plateau Tonga.* Manchester: Manchester University Press.

CONVERSE, H. M. 1908 *Myths and Legends of the New York State Iroquois.* Arthur C. Parker, ed. New York State Museum Bulletin No. 125. Albany, N.Y.

COON, C. S. 1971 *The Hunting Peoples.* New York: Little, Brown.

COULT, A., AND R. W. HABENSTEIN 1965 *Cross-Tabulation of Murdock's World Ethnographic Sample.* Columbia: University of Missouri Press.

DA MATTA, R. 1973 "A Reconsideration of Apinayé Social Morphology," in D. R. Gross, ed., *Peoples and Cultures of Native South America.* Garden City, N.Y.: Natural History Press.

DAS, T. 1945 *The Purums: An Old Kuki Tribe of Manipur.* Calcutta: University of Calcutta.

DAVENPORT, W. 1959 "Nonunilinear Descent and Descent Groups," *American Anthropologist*, 61:557–572.

DAVILA, M. 1971 "Compadrazgo: Fictive Kinship in Latin America," in N. H. H. Graburn, ed., *Readings in Kinship and Social Structure.* New York: Harper & Row.

DOUGLAS, M. 1966 *Purity and Danger.* Baltimore: Penguin.

——. 1970 *Natural Symbols: Explorations in Cosmology.* London: Cresset.

DRIVER, H. 1966 "Geographical-Historical versus Psycho-Functional Explanation of Kin Avoidance," *Current Anthropology*, 7:131–160; 176–182.

DRIVER, H., AND K. F. SCHUESSLER 1967 "Correlational Analysis of Murdock's 1957 Ethnographic Sample," *American Anthropologist*, 69:332–352.

DUMONT, L. 1953 "The Dravidian Kinship Terminology as an Expression of Marriage," *Man*, 53:34–39.

———. 1957 *Hierarchy and Marriage Alliance in South Indian Kinship*. Occasional Paper of the Royal Anthropological Institute No. 12.

———. 1968 "Marriage Alliance," *International Encyclopedia of Social Science*, 10:19–23.

DURKHEIM, E. 1912 *Les Formes Élémentaires de la Vie Religieuse*. Paris: Presses Universitaires. (Trans. by J. R. Swain as *The Elementary Forms of Religious Life*. New York: Free Press, 1954.)

EGGAN, F. 1937 "Historical Changes in the Choctaw Kinship System," *American Anthropologist*, 37:34–52.

———. 1968 "Kinship," *International Encyclopedia of Social Science*, 8:390–401.

———. 1972 "Lewis Henry Morgan's *Systems*: A Re-evaluation," in P. Reining, ed., *Kinship Studies in the Morgan Centennial Year*. Washington, D.C.: Anthropological Society of Washington.

EVANS-PRITCHARD, E. E. 1940 *The Nuer*. Oxford: Clarendon Press.

———. 1951 *Kinship and Marriage among the Nuer*. Oxford: Clarendon Press.

———. 1956 *Nuer Religion*. Oxford: Clarendon Press.

FENTON, WILLIAM N. 1951 "Locality as a Basic Factor in the Development of Iroquois Social Structure," in W. Fenton, ed., *Symposium on Local Diversity in Iroquois Culture*. Bureau of American Ethnology Bulletin No. 149. Washington, D.C.: U.S. Government Printing Office.

FIRTH, R. 1936 *We the Tikopia*. London: G. Allen.

———. 1957 "A Note on Descent Groups in Polynesia," *Man*, 57:4–8.

———. 1963 "Bilateral Descent Groups: An Operational Viewpoint," in I. Schapera, ed., *Studies in Kinship and Marriage*, R.A.I. Paper 16.

FORDE, C. D. 1950 "Double Descent among the Yako," in A. R. Radcliffe-Brown and C. D. Forde, eds., *African Systems of Kinship and Marriage*. London: Oxford University Press.

———. 1963 "On Some Further Unconsidered Aspects of Descent," *Man*, 63:12–13.

FORTES, M. 1945 *The Dynamics of Clanship among the Tallensi*. London: Oxford University Press.

———. 1949 *The Web of Kinship among the Tallensi*. London: Oxford University Press.

———. 1953 "The Structure of Unilineal Descent Groups," *American Anthropologist*, 55:17–41.

———. 1959a "Primitive Kinship," *Scientific American*, 200, 6:146–157.

———. 1959b "Descent, Filiation, and Affinity," *Man*, 59:193–97; 206–12.

———. 1960 "Ancestor Worship in Africa," in M. Fortes and G. Dieterlen, eds., *African Systems of Thought*. International Africa Institute. London: Oxford University Press.

———. 1969 *Kinship and the Social Order: The Legacy of L. H. Morgan*. Chicago: Aldine.

FORTUNE, R. 1932a *Sorcerers of Dobu*. London: Routledge.

———. 1932b "Incest," in *Encyclopedia of the Social Sciences*, 6:620. New York: Macmillan.

FRAKE, C. O. 1960 "The Eastern Subanun of Mindanao," in G. P. Murdock, ed.,

Social Structure in Southeast Asia. Viking Fund Publications in Anthropology, 29. New York: Wenner-Gren.

FREEMAN, J. D. 1955 *Iban Agriculture.* Colonial Research Studies No. 18. London: Colonial Office.

———. 1958 "The Family System of the Iban of Borneo," in J. Goody, ed., *The Developmental Cycle in Domestic Groups.* Cambridge Papers in Social Anthropology. Cambridge, England: Cambridge University Press.

———. 1960 "The Iban of Borneo," in G. P. Murdock, ed., *Social Structure in Southeast Asia.* Viking Fund Publications in Anthropology, 29. New York: Wenner-Gren.

———. 1961 "On the Concept of the Kindred," *Journal of the Royal Anthropological Institute,* 91:192–220.

———. 1969 "Human Nature and Culture," in *Man and the New Biology.* Canberra: Australian National University Press.

———. 1974 "Kinship, Attachment Behaviour and the Primary Bond," in J. R. Goody, ed., *The Character of Kinship.* Cambridge, England: Cambridge University Press.

FUSTEL DE COULANGES, N. D. 1864 *Le Cité Antique.* (Trans. by W. Small as *The Ancient City.* New York: Doubleday Anchor.)

GEERTZ, C. 1959 "Form and Variation in Balinese Village Structure," *American Anthropologist,* 61:991–1012.

GIFFORD, E. W. 1929 *Tongan Society.* Bernice P. Bishop Museum Bulletin No. 61. Honolulu.

GLICKMAN, M. 1972 "The Nuer and the Dinka: A Further Note," *Man* (n.s.), 7:586–594.

GLUCKMAN, M. 1953 "Bridewealth and the Stability of Marriage," *Man,* 53:141–142.

GOLDENWEISER, A. A. 1910 "Totemism: An Analytical Study," *Journal of American Folklore,* 23:1–115.

GOODALE, J. C. 1962 "Marriage Contracts among the Tiwi," *Ethnology,* 1:452–466.

———. 1971 *Tiwi Wives: A Study of the Women of Melville Island, North Australia.* American Ethnological Society Monograph No. 51. Seattle: University of Washington Press.

GOODENOUGH, W. 1951 *Property, Kin and Community on Truk.* Yale University Publications in Anthropology, 46. New Haven, Conn.

———. 1955 "A Problem in Malayo-Polynesian Social Organization," *American Anthropologist,* 57:71–83.

———. 1956 "Residence Rules," *Southwestern Journal of Anthropology,* 12:22–37.

———. 1961 "Comment on Cultural Evolution," *Daedalus,* 90:521–528.

———. 1962 "Kindred and Hamlet in Lakalai, New Britain," *Ethnology,* 1:5–12.

———. 1968 "Componential Analysis," *International Encyclopedia of the Social Sciences,* 3:186–192.

———. 1970 *Description and Comparison in Cultural Anthropology.* Lewis Henry Morgan Lectures, 1968. Chicago: Aldine.

GOODY, J. R. 1959 "The Mother's Brother and the Sister's Son in West Africa," *Journal of the Royal Anthropological Institute,* 89, 1:61–88.

———. 1961 "The Classification of Double Descent Systems," *Current Anthropology,* 2, 1:3–12.

————. 1968 "Kinship: Descent Groups," *International Encyclopedia of the Social Sciences*, 8:401–408.

————. 1969 *Comparative Studies in Kinship*. Stanford: Stanford University Press.

————. 1971 *Kinship: Selected Readings*. Baltimore: Penguin.

————. 1972 *Domestic Groups*. Addison-Wesley Modules in Social Anthropology. Reading, Mass.: Addison-Wesley.

————. 1974 ed. *The Character of Kinship*. Cambridge, England: Cambridge University Press.

GOODY, J. R., AND S. N. TAMBIAH, eds. 1973 *Bridewealth and Dowry*. Cambridge, England: Cambridge University Press.

GOUGH, K. 1961 "Variation in Matrilineal Systems," Part 2 of D. Schneider and K. Gough, eds., *Matrilineal Kinship*. Berkeley: University of California Press.

————. 1971 "Nuer Kinship and Marriage: A Reexamination," in T. Beidelman, ed., *The Translation of Culture*. London: Tavistock.

GRABURN, N. H. H. 1971 *Readings in Kinship and Social Structure*. New York: Harper & Row.

GREUEL, P. J. 1971 "The Leopard-Skin Chief: An Examination of Political Power among the Nuer," *American Anthropologist*, 73:1115–1120.

HAIGHT, B. 1972 "A Note on the Leopard-Skin Chief," *American Anthropologist*, 74:1313–1318.

HARRIS, M. 1968 *The Rise of Anthropological Theory*. New York: Crowell.

HOCART, A. M. 1937 "Kinship Systems," *Anthropos*, 32:345–351.

HOGBIN, H. I. 1963 *Kinship and Marriage in a New Guinea Village*. London: Athlone.

————. 1964 *A Guadalcanal Society: The Kaoka Speakers*. New York: Holt, Rinehart and Winston, Inc.

HOGBIN, H. I., AND C. WEDGEWOOD 1953 "Local Grouping in Melanesia," *Oceania*, 23:241–276; 24:58–76.

HOMANS, G. C., AND D. SCHNEIDER 1955 *Marriage, Authority and Final Causes*. Glencoe, Illinois: Free Press.

KAEPPLER, A. L. 1971 "Rank in Tonga," *Ethnology*, 10, 2:174–193.

KEESING, R. M. 1966 "Kwaio Kindreds," *Southwestern Journal of Anthropology*, 22, 4:346–353.

————. 1967 "Statistical Models and Decision Model of Social Structure: A Kwaio Case," *Ethnology*, 6:1–16.

————. 1968a "On Descent and Descent Groups," *Current Anthropology*, 9:453–454.

————. 1968b "Nonunilineal Descent and the Contextual Definition of Status," *American Anthropologist*, 70:82–84.

————. 1969 "On Quibblings over Squabblings of Siblings: New Perspectives on Kin Terms and Role Behaviour," *Southwestern Journal of Anthropology*, 25:207–227.

————. 1970 "Shrines, Ancestors, and Cognatic Descent: The Kwaio and Tallensi," *American Anthropologist*, 72:755–775.

————. 1971 "Descent, Residence, and Cultural Codes," in L. Hiatt and C. Jayarwardena, eds., *Anthropology in Oceania*. Sydney: Angus and Robertson.

————. 1972 "Simple Models of Complexity: The Lure of Kinship," in P. Reining, ed., *Kinship Studies in the Morgan Centennial Year*. Washington,
D.C.: Anthropological Society of Washington.

KEESING, R. M., AND F. M. KEESING 1971 *New Perspectives in Cultural Anthropology*. New York: Holt, Rinehart and Winston, Inc.

KÖBBEN, A. J. F. 1967 "Why Exceptions? The Logic of Cross-Cultural Comparison," *Current Anthropology*, 8:3–34.

KOPYTOFF, I. 1964 "Family and Lineage among the Suku of the Congo," in R. F.
Gray and P. H. Gulliver, eds., *The Family Estate in Africa*. London:
Routledge.

————. 1965 "The Suku of Southwestern Congo," in J. Gibbs, Jr., ed., *Peoples
of Africa*. New York: Holt, Rinehart and Winston, Inc.

————. 1971 "Ancestors as Elders in Africa," *Africa*, 41, 11:129–142.

KORN, F. 1973 *Elementary Structures Reconsidered: Lévi-Strauss on Kinship*.
Berkeley: University of California Press.

LANGNESS, L. L. 1964 "Some Problems in the Conceptualization of Highlands
Social Structure," in J. Watson, ed., *The New Guinea Highlands. American
Anthropologist*, 66,4, Part 2:162–182.

LAWRENCE, W. E., 1937 "Alternate Generations in Australia," in G. P. Murdock,
ed., *Studies in the Science of Society*. New Haven: Yale University Press.

LEACH, E. R. 1945 "Jinghpaw Kinship Terminology," *Journal of the Royal Anthropological Institute*, 75:59–72.

————. 1953 "Bridewealth and the Stability of Marriage," *Man*, 53:179–180.

————. 1954 *Political Systems of Highland Burma*. Cambridge, Mass.: Harvard
University Press.

————. 1955 "Polyandry, Inheritance and the Definition of Marriage," *Man*,
55:182–186.

————. 1957 "Aspects of Bridewealth and Marriage Stability among the Kachin
and Lakher," *Man*, 57:59.

————. 1958 "Concerning Trobriand Clans and the Kinship Category *Tabu*," in
J. R. Goody, ed., *The Developmental Cycle of Domestic Groups*. Cambridge Papers in Social Anthropology, 1.

————. 1961 *Pul Eliya*. Cambridge, England: Cambridge University Press.

————. 1962a "On Certain Unconsidered Aspects of Double Descent," *Man*,
62:130–134.

————. 1962b *Rethinking Anthropology*. London: Athlone.

————. 1970 *Lévi-Strauss*. Fontana Modern Masters Series. London: Collins.

LEE, R., AND I. DEVORE, eds. 1968 *Man the Hunter*. Chicago: Aldine.

LÉVI-STRAUSS, C. 1949 *Les Structures Élémentaires de la Parenté*. Paris: Plon.
(Trans. by J. Bell, J. Von Sturmer, and R. Needham as *Elementary Structures of Kinship*. Boston: Beacon Press, 1969.)

————. 1956 "The Family," in H. L. Shapiro, ed., *Man, Culture, and Society*.
New York: Oxford University Press.

————. 1962 *Totémisme Aujourd'hui*. (Trans. by R. Needham as *Totemism*.
Boston: Beacon Press, 1963.)

————. 1963 "Do Dual Organizations Exist," in C. Lévi-Strauss, *Structural
Anthropology*. Paris: Plon.

————. 1966 "The Future of Kinship Studies," *Proceedings of the Royal Anthropological Institute* (1965):13–22.

LI AN-CHE 1937 "Zuni: Some Observations and Queries," *American Anthropologist,* 39:62–76.

LIENHARDT, G. 1961 *Divinity and Experience: The Religion of the Dinka.* Oxford, England: Clarendon Press.

LOUNSBURY, F. G. 1962 Review of R. Needham, *Structure and Sentiment. American Anthropologist,* 64:1302–1310.

———. 1964a "A Formal Account of the Omaha- and Crow-Type Kinship Terminologies," in W. Goodenough, ed., *Explorations in Cultural Anthropology.* New York: McGraw-Hill.

———. 1964b "The Structural Analysis of Kinship Semantics," in H. E. Hunt, ed., *Proceedings of the Ninth International Congress of Linguists.* The Hague: Mouton.

———. 1965 "Another View of the Trobriand Kinship Categories," in E. A. Hammel, ed., *Formal Semantic Analysis.* American Anthropologist Special Publications, 67, 5, Part 2.

LOWIE, R. H. 1915 "Exogamy and the Classificatory Systems of Relationship," *American Anthropologist,* 17:223–239.

———. 1928 "Relationship Terms," *Encyclopedia Britannica,* 19:84–90. (Reprinted in J. Middleton and P. Bohannan, eds., *Kinship and Social Organization.* New York: Natural History Press.)

MALINOWSKI, B. 1922 *Argonauts of the Western Pacific,* London: Routledge.

———. 1929 *The Sexual Life of Savages in Northwestern Melanesia.* London: Routledge.

———. 1935 *Coral Gardens and their Magic.* 2 vols. London: G. Allen.

MARSHALL, G. A. 1968 "Marriage: Comparative Analysis," *International Encyclopedia of the Social Sciences,* 10:8–19.

MARSHALL, L. 1959 "Marriage among the !Kung Bushmen," *Africa,* 29:335–364.

———. 1960 "!Kung Bushmen Bands," *Africa,* 30:325–355.

———. 1965 "The !Kung Bushmen of the Kalahari Desert," in J. Gibbs, Jr., ed., *Peoples of Africa.* New York: Holt, Rinehart and Winston, Inc.

MAYBURY-LEWIS, D. H. P. 1960 "Parallel Descent and the Apinayé Anomaly," *Southwestern Journal of Anthropology,* 16:191–216.

———. 1965 "Prescriptive Marriage Systems," *Southwestern Journal of Anthropology,* 21:207–230.

———. 1967 Akwe-Shavante Society. London: Oxford University Press.

MEAD, M. 1935 *Sex and Temperament in Three New Guinea Societies.* New York: Morrow.

MIDDLETON, J., AND D. TAIT 1958 "Introduction," in J. Middleton and D. Tait, *Tribes Without Rulers.* London: Routledge.

MINTZ, S., AND E. R. WOLF 1950 "An Analysis of Ritual Co-Parenthood (Compadrazgo)," *Southwestern Journal of Anthropology,* 6:341–368.

MITCHELL, J. C. 1969 "The Concept and Use of Social Networks," in J. C. Mitchell, ed., *Social Networks in Urban Situations.* 2d ed. Manchester, England: Manchester University Press.

MITCHELL, W. E. 1963 "Theoretical Problems in the Concept of the Kindred," *American Anthropologist,* 65:343–354.

MORGAN, L. H. 1851 *League of the Ho-De-No-Sau-Nee or Iroquois.* Reprint. New York: Dodd, Mead, 1904.

MURDOCK, G. P. 1949 *Social Structure.* New York: Macmillan.

———. 1957 "World Ethnographic Sample," *American Anthropologist*, 59:664–687.

———. 1959 "Evolution in Social Organization," in B. J. Meggers, ed., *Evolution and Anthropology*. Washington: Anthropological Society of Washington.

———. 1960 "Cognatic Form of Social Organization," in G. P. Murdock, ed., *Social Structure in Southeast Asia*. Viking Fund Publications in Anthropology, 29. New York: Wenner-Gren.

———. 1967 *Ethnographic Atlas*. Pittsburgh: University of Pittsburgh Press.

NADEL, S. F. 1950 "Dual Descent in the Nuba Hills," in A. R. Radcliffe-Brown and C. F. Forde, eds., *African Systems of Kinship and Marriage*. London: Oxford University Press.

NAROLL, R. 1970 "Galton's Problem," in R. Naroll and R. Cohen, eds., *A Handbook of Method in Cultural Anthropology*. Garden City, N.Y.: Natural History Press.

NAROLL, R. AND R. COHEN, eds. 1970 *A Handbook of Method in Cultural Anthropology*. Garden City, N.Y.: Natural History Press.

NEEDHAM, R. 1962a *Structure and Sentiment: A Test Case in Social Anthropology*. Chicago: University of Chicago Press.

———. 1962b "Genealogy and Category in Wikmunkan Society," *Ethnology*, 1:223–264.

———. 1972 "Remarks on the Analysis of Kinship and Marriage," in R. Needham, ed., *Kinship and Marriage*, ASA Monograph, 11. London: Tavistock.

———. 1973 *Right and Left: Essays on Dual Symbolic Classification*. Chicago: University of Chicago Press.

NEWCOMER, P. J. 1972 "The Nuer are Dinka: An Essay on Origins and Environmental Determinism," *Man* (n.s.), 7:5–11.

NIMUENDAJÚ, C. 1939 *The Apinayé*. 2d ed. (Trans. by R. Lowie. New York: Humanities Press, 1967.)

OPLER, M. E. 1937 "Apache Data Concerning the Relations of Kinship Terminology to Social Classification," *American Anthropologist*, 39:201–212.

PARKINSON, C. N. 1957 *Parkinson's Law*. Boston: Houghton Mifflin.

PASTNER, S. 1971 "Camels, Sheep and Nomad Social Organization: A Comment on Rubel's Model," *Man* (n.s.), 6:285–288.

PEHRSON, R. N. 1954 "Bilateral Kin Groupings as a Structural Type," *Journal of East Asiatic Studies*, 3:199–202.

———. 1957 *The Bilateral Network of Social Relations in Könkämä Lapp District*. Bloomington: Indiana University Research Center in Anthropology, Folklore and Linguistics.

PERANIO, R. D. 1961 "Descent, Descent Line, and Descent Group in Cognatic Social Systems," *Proceedings of the 1961 Annual Spring Meeting of the American Ethnological Society*, 93–113.

POWELL, H. A. 1960 "Competitive Leadership in Trobriand Political Organization," *Journal of the Royal Anthropological Institute*, 90:118–145.

———. 1969a "Genealogy, Residence and Kinship in Kiriwina," *Man*, (4)2:117–202.

———. 1969b "Territory, Hierarchy and Kinship in Kiriwina," *Man*, (4)4:580–604.

RADCLIFFE-BROWN, A. R. 1913 "Three Tribes of Western Australia," *Journal of the Royal Anthropological Institute*, 43:143–194.

———. 1941 "The Study of Kinship Systems," *Journal of the Royal Anthropological Institute*, 71:1–18.

———. 1924 "The Mother's Brother in South Africa," in A. R. Radcliffe-Brown, ed., *Structure and Function in Primitive Society*. London: Cohen and West, Reprinted 1952.

———. 1930 "The Social Organization of Australian Tribes," *Oceania*, 1:34–63.

———. 1950 "Introduction," in A. R. Radcliffe-Brown and C. D. Forde, eds., *African Systems of Kinship and Marriage*. London: Oxford University Press.

———. 1951 "The Comparative Method in Social Anthropology," *Journal of the Royal Anthropological Institute*, 81:15–22.

RANDLE, M. C. 1951 "Iroquois Women, Then and Now," in W. N. Fenton, ed., *Symposium on Local Diversity in Iroquois Culture*. Bureau of American Ethnology Bulletin No. 149. Washington, D.C.: U.S. Government Printing Office.

RAPPAPORT, R. 1971 "Ritual, Sanctity, and Cybernetics," *American Anthropologist*, 73:59–76.

RICHARDS, A. I. 1950 "Some Types of Family Structure amongst the Central Bantu," in A. R. Radcliffe-Brown and C. D. Forde, eds., *African Systems of Kinship and Marriage*. London: Oxford University Press.

RICHARDS, C. 1957 "Matriarchy or Mistake: The Role of Iroquois Women through Time," in *Cultural Stability and Cultural Change*. Proceedings of the 1957 Annual Meeting of the American Ethnological Society. Seattle, Washington: University of Washington Press.

ROBINSON, M. 1962 "Complementary Filiation and Marriage in the Trobriand Islands," in M. Fortes, ed., *Marriage in Tribal Societies*. Cambridge Papers in Social Anthropology, 3. London: Cambridge University Press.

ROMNEY, A. K., AND P. EPLING 1958 "A Simplified Model of Kariera Kinship," *American Anthropologist*, 60:59–74.

RUBEL, P. 1969 "Herd Composition and Social Structure: On Building Models of Nomadic Pastoral Societies," *Man* (n.s.), 4:268–273.

SAHLINS, M. 1958 *Social Stratification in Polynesia*. American Ethnological Society. Seattle: University of Washington Press.

———. 1960 "Evolution, Specific and General," in M. Sahlins and E. Service, eds., *Evolution and Culture*. Ann Arbor: University of Michigan Press.

———. 1961 "The Segmentary Lineage: An Organization of Predatory Expansion," *American Anthropologist*, 63:322–345.

———. 1962 *Moala: Culture and Nature on a Fijian Island*. Ann Arbor: University of Michigan Press.

———. 1965 "On the Ideology and Composition of Descent Groups," *Man*, 65:104–107.

———. 1968 *Tribesmen*. Englewood Cliffs, N.J.: Prentice-Hall.

SCHEFFLER, H. W. 1964 "Descent Concepts and Descent Groups: The Maori Case," *Journal of the Polynesian Society*, 73:126–133.

———. 1965 *Choiseul Island Social Structure*. Berkeley: University of California Press.

————. 1966 "Ancestor Worship in Anthropology: Observations on Descent and Descent Groups," *Current Anthropology*, 7:54–98.

————. 1970 " 'The Elementary Structures of Kinship' by C. Lévi-Strauss: A Review Article," *American Anthropologist*, 72:251–68.

————. 1971 "Dravidian-Iroquois: The Melanesian Evidence," in L. Hiatt and C. Jayarwardena, eds., *Anthropology in Oceania*. Sydney: Angus and Robertson.

————. 1972a "Kinship Semantics," in B. Siegel, ed., *Annual Reviews of Anthropology*. Palo Alto, Calif.: Annual Reviews, Inc.

————. 1972b "Systems of Kin Classification: A Structural Semantic Typology," in P. Reining, ed., *Kinship Studies in the Morgan Centennial Year*. Washington, D.C.: Anthropological Society of Washington.

————. 1974 "Kinship, Descent and Alliance," in J. J. Honigmann, ed., *Handbook of Social and Cultural Anthropology*. New York: Rand McNally.

———— n.d. "Australian System of Kin Classification; Part I: Kariera-Like Systems." Unpublished manuscript.

SCHEFFLER, H. W., AND F. LOUNSBURY 1971 *A Study in Structural Semantics: The Siriono Kinship System*. Englewood Cliffs, N.J.: Prentice-Hall.

SCHNEIDER, D. M. 1961 "Introduction" in D. Schneider and K. Gough, eds., *Matrilineal Kinship*. Berkeley: University of California Press.

————. 1965 "Some Muddles in the Models: or, How the System Really Works," in M. Banton, ed., *The Relevance of Models in Social Anthropology*. ASA Monographs, 1. London: Tavistock.

————. 1968 *American Kinship: A Cultural Account*. Englewood Cliffs, N.J.: Prentice-Hall.

————. 1972 "What is Kinship All About?" in P. Reining, ed., *Kinship Studies in the Morgan Centennial Year*. Washington, D.C.: Anthropological Society of Washington.

SCHNEIDER, D., AND K. GOUGH, eds. 1961 *Matrilineal Kinship*. Berkeley: University of California Press.

SCHNEIDER, D., AND R. SMITH. 1973 *Class Differences and Sex Roles in American Kinship*. Englewood Cliffs, N.J.: Prentice-Hall.

SERVICE, E. 1966 *The Hunters*. Englewood Cliffs, N.J.: Prentice-Hall.

SHAPIRO, W. 1970 "Local Exogamy and the Wife's Mother in Aboriginal Australia," in R. Berndt, ed., *Australian Aboriginal Anthropology*. Nedlands, Australia: University of Western Australia Press.

SILVERMAN, M. G. 1971 *Disconcerting Issue: Meaning and Struggle in a Resettled Pacific Community*. Chicago: University of Chicago Press.

SMITH, M. G. 1956 "On Segmentary Lineage Systems," *Journal of the Royal Anthropological Institute*, 86:39–79.

SPOEHR, A. 1947 "Changing Kinship Systems," Field Museum of Natural History Publications 583, Anthropological Series 33:151–235.

STEWARD, J. 1955 *Theory of Culture Change*. Urbana, Ill.: University of Illinois Press.

STRATHERN, A. J. 1968 "Descent and Alliance in the New Guinea Highlands: Some Problems of Comparison." *Proceedings of the Royal Anthropological Institute*, 37–52.

————. 1972 *One Father, One Blood*. Canberra: Australian National University Press.

TAX, S. 1937 "Some Problems of Social Organization," in F. Eggan, ed., *Social Anthropology of the North American Tribes*. Chicago: University of Chicago Press.

TERRAY, E. 1972 "Historical Materialism and Segmentary Lineage-Based Societies," in E. Terray *Marxism and Primitive Societies*. New York: Monthly Review Press.

TEXTOR, R. 1967 *A Cross-Cultural Summary*. New Haven, Conn.: Human Relations Area Files Press.

THURNWALD, R. 1916 *Bánaro Society: Social Organization and Kinship System of a Tribe in the Interior of New Guinea*. American Anthropological Association Memoir 3, No. 2. Lancaster, Pa.: New Era Printing Company.

TURNER, V. 1957 *Schism and Continuity in an African Society: A Study of Ndembu Village Life*. Manchester: Manchester University Press.

TYLOR, E. 1889 "On a Method of Investigating the Development of Institutions; applied to Laws of Marriage and Descent," *Journal of the Royal Anthropological Institute*, 18:245–269.

WATSON, J., ed. 1965 *The New Guinea Highlands*. American Anthropological Special Publications, Vol. 67.

WHITE, L. A. 1948 "The Definition and Prohibition of Incest," *American Anthropologist*, 50:416–434.

———. 1959 *The Evolution of Culture*. New York: McGraw-Hill.

WHITTEN, N. E., JR., AND D. S. WHITTEN 1972 "Social Strategies and Social Relationships," in B. J. Siegel et al., eds., *Annual Review of Anthropology*, Vol. 1. Palo Alto, Calif.: Annual Reviews.

YALMAN, N. 1962 "The Structure of the Sinhalese Kindred: A Re-Examination of the Dravidian Terminology," *American Anthropologist*, 64:548–575.

———. 1967 *Under the Bo Tree: Studies in Caste, Kinship and Marriage in the Interior of Ceylon*. Berkeley: University of California.

INDEX

NAME INDEX

SUBJECT INDEX

A

Adaptation, of forms of social organization, 4–5, 7, 15–17, 19–20, 25–26, 33, 55–56, 123–124, 134–142
Adoption, 12–13, 71, 129–130
Affinity, 6, 7, 22, 43–45, 88–90, 107, 108–109, 110, 117–118
Africa, social organization in, 20–21, 32–33, 35, 36–38, 49–53, 58–59, 60, 70, 71–75, 89–90, 97
Age, in kinship relations, 54–55, 95, 111–112, 128, 142
Alliance, 45, 78–90, 108–110, 117–118
  asymmetrical, 84–89, 117–118
  symmetrical, 79–84, 108
  versus "descent theory", 89–90
Alliance systems, 5, 45, 78–90, 108, 110, 117

Ancestors, 15, 17, 18, 20, 21, 22, 29, 35, 47, 59–60, 70, 80, 88, 93, 95, 128
Apinayé (Brazil), 76–77
Aranda (Australia), 83
Australian Aborigines, 12–15, 60, 75–76, 77, 79–84

B

Balinese, 45
Bedouin, 45, 96
Bilateral kinship (see Kinship)
Bridewealth, 43, 46, 88–89, 97

C

Caribbean, 35
Castes, 53, 129